Volume 2

REAL WOMEN WRITE

Beyond COVID: Leaning Into Tomorrow

FOREWORD BY
Christina Baldwin

EDITED BY
Susan Schoch

**SHARING STORIES, SHARING LIVES
IN PROSE AND POETRY FROM
STORY CIRCLE NETWORK**

A Publication of Story Circle Network

Real Women Write
Beyond COVID: Leaning Into Tomorrow
Volume 20, 2021

Sharing Stories, Sharing Lives
in Prose and Poetry from Story Circle Network

ISBN: 978-0-9795329-8-6

Story Circle Network
723 W University Ave #300-234
Georgetown TX 78626

https://www.storycircle.org

Real Women Write is a series of annual anthologies, each exploring a theme of significance to all women through the nonfiction, fiction, and poetry of Story Circle Network members. It appears in December, in both print and digital formats, and showcases the talent and creativity of SCN's writing women.

Story Circle Network values every woman's story. In *Real Women Write* we publish writing about both the uniquely individual life and a woman's life as it's understood by all women.

Foreword by Christina Baldwin

Edited by Susan Schoch

Cover image, interior design, and technical support by Sherry Wachter

"I've got some bad news and I've got some good news.

Nothing lasts forever."

— KATE McGAHAN

"We are, or will be, going through the most radical transformation

the world has ever seen; people are justly terrified, excited,

depressed, heartbroken and hopeful, all at once."

— HEATHER MARSH

CONTENTS

FOREWORD
Christina Baldwin

Soon to be a major motion picture! Covid 19—the Never-ending Story!

"When you go out and see the empty streets,
the empty stadiums, the empty train platforms,
don't say to yourself, 'It looks like the end of the world.'
What you're seeing is love in action.
What you're seeing, in that negative space,
is how much we do care for each other…

People will lose jobs over this.
Some will lose their businesses.
And some will lose their lives.
All the more reason to take a moment…
to look into the emptiness and marvel at all of that love.
Let it fill you and sustain you.
It isn't the end of the world.
It is the most remarkable act of
global solidarity we may ever witness."

— FROM THE BELFAST CORONA VIRUS NETWORK

People like events: things that occur with a beginning/middle/end. We like a good story, or a sporting contest (who won—and we know the score), or a family reunion when all our relatives leave on Tuesday and we can "put things back to rights," as my mother used to say.

When the Covid-19 Pandemic started, it was articulated as an event, a huge global occurrence playing out on the world stage. The virus a sneaky monster, we watched in astonishment as the modern world came to a sudden halt. It felt like we were all living in a disaster movie, complete with spooky music and escalated voices on the news. Lots of real-life drama was generated in Act One watching healthcare systems near to collapsing under the load of need, and heartfelt relief was provided by stories and gestures of kindness and support.

But now, in its second year of ongoing disruption, the pandemic is not behaving properly. The plot is very unclear, unmanageable subplots are bobbing like container ships at the edges of ports. The story needs serious editing. It seems stuck in what my editor refers to as "the muddle of the middle." Well, if we are even in the middle. And in the early summer of 2021, just when the vaccinated were dashing toward the exits and a promised return to normalcy, the Delta variant cancelled Intermission. Anti-vaxxers cancelled civility. Misinformation cancelled confidence. We don't know where we are or how to live our ways forward. We are certainly in the muddle!

Oh, a new reality is dawning. The pandemic is not an event: the pandemic is a *shift*.

A shift is a much harder experience. We don't know how long it is, how big it is, or what consequences it enforces. We don't know if it actually ever comes to a resolution in which the protagonists have triumphed, good has won the day, the dust-up of drama has settled, and we can finish our popcorn and eye the satisfying announcement, THE END… In a shift, is the end just THE BEGINNING? And beginning of what? And what just ended? And who am I in the muddle of this? How can I make story and meaning when everything keeps changing? And what happened to the camaraderie when we were cheering for team humanity?

I want opera on the balconies again and clanging pans for nurses, and poetry about togetherness, and thoughtful pieces about how this might change our lives for the better. I want to believe that beautiful declaration of the Belfast Corona Virus Network, "It isn't the end of the world. It is the most remarkable act of global solidarity we may ever witness."

All this range of confusion is brought to the pages of this anthology. Each woman's voice is a glittering piece in the kaleidoscope of pandemic shifting. These essays, poetry, and mini-memoirs are captured moments of artistic task: the determination to shape meaning in a situation where meaning is constantly in shift. A Spanish proverb that has guided me for many years says: There is no path; we make the path by walking. In the New Now of the pandemic and polycrises: There is no story; we make the story by writing and talking.

Returning to teaching my memoir and autobiography seminar, sitting in a circle of earnest and dedicated writers for the first time in two years, we spent the first morning articulating the significance of what we have lived through while waiting for this class to reconvene.

Phrases tumbled out of us: ...*my life is life divided into BC (Before Covid) and DC (During Covid) and I don't know if there is an AC (After Covid)... the story I was writing for my grandchildren now seems irrelevant to me, and to them... I am tongue-tied, and thunder-struck, and spinning in place... I open my journal and stare at the blank page; I don't know what to say to myself.*

At some point in our check-in, a woman asks, *"But isn't confusion itself a narrative? And if so, can't we braid confusion into stories that can carry us through?"* Yes. And it's a greater challenge because there is no solid ground for the story to stand on. Nothing is historical.

Yet the stories in this anthology are just such a weave and they do help carry us through. These stories and poems show us the braid of our resilience. They help us remember and honor the essential acts of goodness that remind us we care about one another. Even when we fall: we get up. Even as we grieve: we celebrate. These are stories that rise out of a moment of pause, but not completion—for we are not complete. These are stories that allow us to companion one another and to companion the shift. There is no path: we make the path through story. In a period of such immense shift, this is what we have: words strong enough to hold us and let us take another step.

Shift.

CHRISTINA BALDWIN
Author of The Circle Way, Storycatcher, The Seven Whispers, Life's Companion, *and other titles, has been a presenter, speaker, and long-time supporter of Story Circle Network. She lives on Whidbey Island in Washington State.* www.peerspirit.com

EDITOR'S NOTE
December 2021

Beyond *COVID: Leaning Into Tomorrow* is Volume 20 in the annual *Real Women Write* anthology series from Story Circle Network.

We ended our 2020 edition, *Living on COVID Time,* with a piece by renowned author and SCN founder Susan Wittig Albert, who pointed us to the challenge ahead: *change.* "A deep breath, a big turn, the long work. And my own pledge to work harder, pay more attention, take more responsibility. And be a part of the unraveling and the reweaving."

In this 2021 issue, we begin with a Foreword by award-winning author, teacher, and activist Christina Baldwin, which extends Susan's look at the work before us. Christina suggests that COVID-19 is not an event, but part of a global *shift,* and we are each shifting in our own way. "There is no path: we make the path through story." Women writers weave and reweave words. We revise our dreams of the future.

Considering the impact of variants like Delta and Omicron, as well as waning vaccine effectiveness, the theme for this issue may have been premature. It is tough to think beyond COVID, or to lean into such an uncertain tomorrow. Back in early 2021, when we chose the topic, it still wasn't clear that the future might not be "beyond COVID" so much as "with COVID." Yet now that reality is evident in the 63 pieces by 53 writers included here.

You will find a remarkable breadth of responses to the theme. Some authors are explicit about the future, others are compelled by the past or absorbed in present drama and not yet looking ahead. For a few, prospects look bleak. Yet others see new freedoms. And for many, there is hope – that we will learn and grow, finding resilience, building community, and appreciating our diversity. Each possibility comes in its unique form and voice. The combined result is an extraordinary chorus, always the surprising strength of a Story Circle Network anthology.

In this issue, we especially celebrate that diversity of voices, because this is the twentieth anniversary edition of our annual member-writers collection. And in 2021, as always, SCN understands that diversity is valuable, necessary, and enriching. Over the years, we have included an enormous range of women's stories and poetry, and *Real Women Write* continues to represent the harmony found in gathering many individual women's experiences into a collection to be shared.

That appreciation for the individual voice means that editing here is light, and some usages may be inconsistent, idiomatic, or occasionally grammatically incorrect. The COVID-19 virus, for example, is also referred to as COVID, covid, Covid, the pandemic, or simply the virus. It does not seem necessary to force consistency on a term that is still under active development. And it doesn't seem necessary to force uniformity in the writing, as long as an author's style is natural and clear, even if not the norm. But author errors like misplaced commas, misspellings, and grammar that may cause confusion have been corrected.

While the anthology includes a generous sampling of entries received, selection is limited. We work hard to choose the best writing – relevant, engaging, worth your time – and also publish writers of varied experience and opportunity.

Editing *Real Women Write* is an honor, and a rewarding and growthful experience, because of the trust and support of the extraordinary women of Story Circle Network. Vital to this project are Susan Wittig Albert; Len Leatherwood; Jeanne Guy; Teresa Lynn; Sherry Wachter; Shelley Carey; and SCN's entire Board of Directors. I am ever thankful for their generous expertise and kind friendship.

We are all grateful for Christina Baldwin's thoughtful interest in this project. Her warm and energetic Foreword roots the collection in profound wisdom, and helps us see the whole in its many parts. Christina is a longtime friend of Story Circle, whose work continues to inform and inspire women writers around the world.

And as always, we are immensely thankful for the contributing authors, who made this book possible. Their creativity, insightful candor, and writing hearts make *Beyond COVID: Leaning Into Tomorrow* an important addition to the herstory of this time.

As we enter the third year of this pandemic, may we move forward together with the hope and resilience reflected in this remarkable collection.

SUSAN SCHOCH, EDITOR
Real Women Write, Volume 20
Beyond COVID: Leaning Into Tomorrow

LEANING INTO TOMORROW?

Jeanne Zeeb-Schecter

The theme for this year's SCN anthology is *Beyond Covid: Leaning into Tomorrow.* I think the focus was picked just at the beginning of the year, when none of us could imagine Covid would still be thrashing around causing chaos and heartache in most of our lives some nine months later, with no end in sight.

I've enjoyed having more quiet time these last eighteen months; I found some inner strength within that quiet that helped me know what I really wanted. I made the decision to retire and make writing my focus. I learned to adapt to the Zoom technology needed to take my writing classes online. Not too shabby for a 77-year-old. I mastered making egg bread—challah—each Friday for our Sabbath meals. I reminded myself countless times that I have a husband that I love and even really like after 34 years together, to go through this last year-and-a-half alongside.

And yet…enough already. I've adjusted, readjusted, and now I want some stability. I want to hug my great-grandchildren and not be concerned because they play basketball and football and one of their teammates or a visiting team member is always testing positive for Covid.

California insisted on lockdowns, but now we can turn on the television and see stadiums and basketball gyms crowded with fans. It's mind-boggling. The news sells fear about how contagious the new Delta variant is, how it can be carried and contracted by the unvaccinated and fully vaccinated as well, and then runs videos of filled sports arenas. People are traveling for pleasure. My mind can't make sense of it. Remember the Sesame Street song that had this line? "One of these things is not like the other."

So how do I write an essay about leaning into tomorrow when none of us know when that tomorrow will be or what it will look like. It's a mystery because we aren't there yet and we don't have an expected due date for that happening. I do know that Covid has made subtle changes within me, apart from retiring, etc. I've been trying to think of how to describe them. It's difficult.

We just went through the 20th anniversary of the 9-11 terrorist attacks. I can easily come up with the words to describe how that changed me. The collective grief we experienced as a nation still lives within me when I watch a new documentary on 9-11. Or when I think about the first responders who are sick and dying because of all the chemicals they were exposed to twenty years ago, the survivors with PTSD and guilt, and the families of the those 2,977 who died. Grief changes you. We were attacked on our soil. The innocence and security that we as a nation once felt are now diminished. The world has felt less safe in my mind since that day in 2001.

But…Covid? How does one lean into the future while a pandemic is still hovering around the world. How naïve do I have to be to believe that things will go back to "normal?" I've lost people to Covid. I have family who have lost friends to suicide during Covid because they were ill-equipped mentally to deal with the loss of their income, the inability to support their children, or were unable to be with their cranky, caged children, day after day at home, unable to go to work where they were listened to and respected by others. I watched their funerals on Zoom, with no physical hugs, no comfort from friends and family. Just masks.

Anger and protests are part of almost everyone's rhetoric today. Political bashing on both sides has been partially replaced with vaccine shaming. If you refuse vaccination, you are a bad person. You're not misguided, you are just inherently bad, even if you stay inside and don't socialize with others. The anger spews out and then ends with, "It's just because I care about you." Really?

I know that for many, anger and hate are easier to feel than grief and fear. It's much more difficult to be depressed when you're angry because it has so much energy behind it. You know you are alive. But now this seems to have become part of America's makeup. Will it leave when we are all "safe" again? I'm not sure.

So, leaning into the future feels fragile at best. I feel we are truly living on the razor's edge. We will survive as a nation, but who will I be? Who will you be?

CORONA CONTROVERSY

Joan Connor

afterlife after covid-19
this poem to address:
coronavirus disease
of 2019
   of 2020
      of 2021
and then what's the rest?

we don't know
they don't know
there's conflict accepting
a conclusive decision
a cloudy vision

about face masks
   about immunity
      about cases documented

do facemasks deliver protection with
or against B-cells, T-cells, antigens?
i want to sound scientific but
have no clue what it all means
   about those vaccines

moderna, johnson & johnson
pfizer-bioNtech
vaccination cards with
boxes to check

because next is the booster
prepare for new chatter
had your booster yet?
and…does it matter?

so i am quite sure this poem
barely addressed: life
   after covid-19
   an unforeseeable scene.

FALSE EQUIVALENCIES

Margaret Dubay Mikus

re: *NY Times Daily Briefing*
    5/21/21
The problem with saying
COVID is on the run
in a big bold headline
is
that we are not done
and for all those longing
and not given to further reading

all those who resisted masking
even during the worst of times
who believe the lies without

noticing the false equivalencies
who cannot or will not
open their hearts and minds

to contain all of us
in all natural created glory
accepting this true and factual

reality

not that I am unaware of
    complexity
or dismissing of past complicity
but if you ask me

I will say to you
it is not over until
all are protected

until long-haul COVID is
    understood
until we know how long
    immunity lasts
until we know how to handle

future variants, and yet
we do not have a crystal ball
nor are likely to get one that
    works

we can only live as best we can
day to day, remembering
even practicing, kindness

DREAD AND GLEE

Charlotte Phillips

On many days over the past eighteen months, I have secretly and guiltily felt gifts of comfort and peace. I often wonder if this is how extroverts always feel in non-COVID times. My husband and I are both introverts. We enjoy each other's company. We enjoy quiet. We are comfortable and, on most days, happy in our home. In many ways, this last eighteen months has been a gift.

We've had a glimpse of what retirement might look like, and we did well. Knowing this is comforting in ways I can't begin to describe. Before, I suspected and hoped. Now, I know, and knowing is wonderful.

With fewer temptations, more family members have found ways to live within their means. Fewer 'loans' have been requested. In addition, our expenses have been reduced by many small eliminations that add up—fuel, road tolls, dry cleaning, nights out. As a result, the A/C failing, followed by failure of the underground electric line that feeds our meter, and then the HOA having a conniption fit over some discolored paint, were all addressed—not stress-free, but close.

The biggest gift for this family of introverts has been the reduction in pressure to participate in large, loud events—pressure to participate in someone else's idea of a good time. The invitations, of course, have been fewer. But the greatest gift is the lack of pressure to accept. To be clear, when we make ourselves join the crowd, we usually have fun. We enjoy the company of others and love seeing friends and family enjoy themselves. We enjoy meeting other writers and talking about writerly things. We enjoy meeting readers and hearing what they love and hate about our latest stories. We love seeing nieces and nephews perform on the stage of their choice. We enjoy the various art and culture festivals, especially when we can go early and leave when the crowds arrive.

Those same pleasurable events can be beyond exhausting—especially when we don't feel free to leave at will. I have not found the words to help extroverts understand that preparing to step into the arena is not fun and exciting. On the contrary, it's incredibly stressful, can fill me with dread to the point that sucking in air is difficult. And, when I do go, the best part is usually returning to our quiet home, where I can savor the memories just made while snuggled in our peaceful setting.

I think the extroverts of the world have been experiencing these same feelings, but in reverse. People who get energy and pleasure from crowd-immersion must be suffering. I hope they are soon free to seek their joy. I also hope they are able to do so with a bit more compassion for those of us dreading the return of pressure to participate in extrovert fun.

Dread.

On the flip side, we have the joy that comes with freedom of the mundane. I am giddy with anticipation of the day when we once again greet each other with visible smiles and hugs. Just thinking of the possibility of running into a maskless acquaintance and being able to recognize them puts a smile on my face. I look forward to the opportunity to shop for my own groceries, and in doing so, discovering some new offering that must be explored. I can't wait to be in my office and have someone pop in and suggest a break—a walk, a chat, a lunch excursion. And the first time that unvaccinated family member calls to announce he's cooking up something scrumptious for dinner and I'm invited, I think I just may arrive at his house before he completes the invite. I'm vibrating with anticipation.

The thought of those denied experiences returning to daily, normal, mundane events, fills me with glee.

Glee.

Dread and glee—two perfect words, seemingly tailor-made for this moment in time.

IN THE MIDST OF COVID

Carol J. Wechsler Blatter

1.
Like unattended weeds, tall,
out of control
expanding like unpruned trees,
multiplying like mosquitos,
moths, flies,
Covid's new Delta proliferates.

2.
Duped, deceived, deluded
disheartened
we believed Covid's
droplets in noses, devilishly
infiltrating lungs, cutting off breathing
ended—finally
it was not to be
Covid, uninvited guest refused to leave
we cried
tears like a tsunami.

3.
Covid's Delta alive, thrives
controlling lives
apart from loved ones
no hugs, no kisses, masked faces again
intimacy not to be.

4.
Surviving in suffocating spaces
like prisoners hiding in our cells
windowless, dark dreary walls
cold floors
scents of stale tobacco,
every day, the same
colors gone.

5.
Helpless sick people
holding onto each rung tightly
a ladder rising to the sky
to stay alive
& fight Covid's wrath.

6
And me, I'm nowhere,
no idea I belong anywhere.
Can I find a place where I pray,
stay safe, solitary, be cautious,
as Covid prevails?

COVID OR NOT, WE ARE AMERICANS

Jennifer Kim-Rankin

It is ironic. After over a year of worrying about COVID and how many different ways it could attack and kill a person, it is not on the top of my worry list as we open up more in 2021. Yes, even with the Delta variant raging in some parts of the United States, the random attacks on Asian Americans are at the forefront of my mind. Some Americans are quick to ignore or forget that Asian Americans are Americans. We are Americans.

In March of 2020, a couple of weeks after the shutdown, I experienced fear that I had never known before. I felt physically threatened for the first time in my life as I searched the empty shelves for wipes and toilet paper at a local grocery store. Three young men followed me around the store. In the beginning, I thought I had imagined things, but I kept running into them at aisle after aisle. Finally, I decided to test them before I found them guilty. I went to the makeup aisle, and there they were. Then I went to the feminine pad aisle, and there they were. With whispers of the China virus permeating the air, I didn't need any more confirmation. I left the grocery store as quickly as possible by walking out behind a large family.

For the next couple of months, I didn't go out much. And when I did, I always had my husband with me. During this time, I found profound comfort in that my son and daughter didn't look Asian. My daughter and I often ran errands together, but I refrained from going out with her in fear of bringing a random attack to her.

About a month later, I was beginning to feel better when the reports of random attacks on Asians began to surface online. No activity was safe from attack, and no gender or age was safe from attack, either. And the latest was the headline on the Yahoo website on July 12th, 2021: *Woman accused of punching 6-year-old Asian boy in Las Vegas charged with hate crime.* I wondered, *how much hate must she have to punch such a little boy? What would or could justify an adult punching a six-year-old child?*

My family and I immigrated to the United States in 1978, and we settled in the San Francisco Bay area. We didn't speak any English, and my parents had to figure things out. The first three years of our immigrant life were the most brutal time of my life, but they also gave me confidence. If I could survive those years, I knew I could survive anything.

In the beginning, we had a hard time renting an apartment, other children teased us with ching-chong sounds, and people butchered our Korean names. But most of that faded away quickly, as we learned to speak English and changed our names to American names. Though difficult, we settled into our American lives comfortably until the 1992 LA Riots.

Korean Americans from Southern California have a unique name for the event, sa-yee-gu. Or 4-2-9, for April 29, when the riots started in the LA area after the announcement of the "not guilty" verdict in the Rodney King case. As the riots spread, the roads leading from Koreatown to surrounding wealthy white neighborhoods were blocked, and lines of defenses were set in place, trapping the residents and barring outside help. This blockade forced most of the rioting in South Central Los Angeles to Koreatown, which was disproportionately damaged more than any other neighborhood in the area. For example, it was reported that almost half of 850 million dollars worth of damage during the riots occurred in Koreatown shops due to unchecked looting and property damage.

As I watched this horror unfold on TV, I was stunned and terrified that the police were nowhere to be seen, and I began to worry about my parents and the shops they owned. Their dry cleaning shop and shoe repair shop were in Oakland, surrounded by more affluent white neighborhoods. Would their shops be attacked?

There were confirmed reports of police driving away from Koreatown as the rioters fired shots and the Korean shop owners who fought to defend their property returned fire. As Korean American radio stations sent out calls for volunteers, many Korean Americans rushed to help those struggling to fight off the attack. What worried me was that there wasn't a large Korean American population in Northern California to come to mutual aid.

We were all on our own. I agonized over thoughts of my terrified mother holed up in her dry cleaning shop, hiding behind a curtain of clothes, and my father hiding behind a partition in his shoe repair shop, clutching a small hammer. For many months, I would calculate the fastest route to my mother's shop from where I worked in San Francisco and how soon I could be there to help her.

Thankfully, my fears of unrest near my parents' shops never materialized, and things didn't change much in Northern California. I don't remember the residual racism or racist attacks reported across the country at the time. Things seemed to return to normal within a reasonably short time, except for those who lived in Koreatown. They were never able to recoup their business losses and struggled to deal with emotional and psychological trauma. Even amid this kind of racial tension, there weren't many brazen attacks on Asian American elderly, women, children, veterans, and men.

So, I started thinking about what would induce an adult to punch a six-year-old child, beat the elderly, or harass women or men? Would an attack similar to Pearl Harbor make this kind of attack on a particular population acceptable to anyone's mind? We all know what happened after the attack on Pearl Harbor. The American government sanctioned confining innocent American citizens of Japanese ancestry in internment camps.

One startling and little-known fact was that the 442nd Infantry Regiment during World War II was *the most decorated in US military history* and was composed almost entirely of second-generation American soldiers of Japanese ancestry. Among its officers was Young Oak Kim, a man of Korean ancestry and one of its combat leaders in Italy and France.

These decorated American soldiers faced overt racism and struggled to help their families rebuild their lives upon return, while living with the burden of the emotional and psychological trauma.

So, why is the COVID pandemic harkening back to the events of the past? Because people are still looking for someone to blame, and the previous American president had done that. It mattered not whether the information was correct or not. It mattered even less that the coronavirus killed without regard to race. It only mattered that the American president called it the China virus, Wuhan virus, Kung flu, etc. Of course, the world has had to deal with bird flu, swine flu, MERS, SARS outbreaks, etc., but none of these outbreaks ushered in an era of racist attacks on one population. The only difference this time was the leadership, and it chills me to the bone.

And like the LA Riots, many of the victims felt that they were on their own. As the attacks took place, doors were closed on them, and many bystanders looked away. We were all alone, again. So, I am fearful of what future leaders of America will induce other Americans to do and that Asian Americans will be left alone to fend for themselves once again.

I hope that COVID will be a thing of the past, and we'll be able to move on to living normal lives soon. But unfortunately, I'm not sure these senseless attacks on Asian Americans will stop anytime soon. That's why I'm walking into post-COVID tomorrow with far more fear than I had pre-COVID yesterday.

PRETTY LITTLE BASTARD

Jane Gragg Lewis

You're so very tiny we can't even see you, but we fear you. You have no brain, they say, but your intelligence seems superior to ours. We think that only brained creatures have intelligence. Maybe we aren't as smart as we like to believe. Maybe you have an intelligence that we just can't understand.

Your invisibility has more than once brought mighty nations to their knees. Just when we believe we have you figured out, you become a shape-shifter, become even more powerful and outsmart us yet again.

I've seen your picture, thanks to that amazing electron microscope. You, with all your pretty crowns. Royalty of your kind. But, really, you're a beautiful little bastard, thinking of no one but yourself. In that respect, maybe we're not so different after all.

People believe that a nuclear war will end the human race. Others believe that an astronomical cataclysm will erase us from the face of the earth. But maybe, just maybe, it will be you – or another of your kind. In your quiet way, will you some day eliminate us? Are you that shortsighted? Maybe the world really will end with a whimper. *

But just remember: you live a borrowed life. If you erase us, you too will die. With a whimper, along with all the rest of us.

* T. S. Elliot, *The Hollow Men*

STILL PANDEMIC, EVOLVING

Margaret Dubay Mikus

Whatever you did
with the time you had
when you couldn't go out
and thought you might
finally clean and organize your desk
or some equally industrious task
but you never got started
and never progressed yet
somehow the weeks passed
into that vast unknown
or anyway more obviously
unknown, and you may have done
some thing, even something original
but often you needed diversion
a distraction from this dystopian movie set
you had somehow wandered into,
now as you put one toe
into the water out there
if you are a wary sort of person
you find the world has changed
or your perception, and
what you took as safe before
what you took for granted
a refuge even
however unwarranted
now scares you as unwise
or is strictly forbidden.
And it is hard to imagine
if not impossible
any kind of new normal.

Moving Forward

JUST IMAGINE

Pat Bean

I inwardly cringe when looking ahead to what the world holds after the Covid pandemic ends – if it ever does, or if it will only be replaced by an even deadlier threat. Not looking that far ahead is what allows me to hang on to my belief that behind every negative there's a silver lining.

This Pollyanna-ish belief has always been there for me, from not getting a promotion but ending up with a job that brought joy to my days; to burning the nightly dinner and getting a rare night out where someone else did the cooking.

But I'm 82 years old, and realistic enough to know that I won't live to see the world I want my great-grandchildren to enjoy. One ruled by peace, caring, acceptance and love, the world John Lennon asked us to *Imagine* fifty years ago: *Imagine all the people living life in peace … You may say I'm a dreamer, But I'm not the only one, I hope someday you'll join us and the world will be as one.*

As a woman born only twenty years after American women could vote, the same year World War II began, and two years before The Great Depression ended, I have seen many great strides forward, including vaccines that erased deadly childhood diseases like smallpox, measles, diphtheria, and polio.

It boggles my mind to watch the polarization of America, fueled by politics, which has resulted in a goodly portion of Americans being unwilling to get a vaccine or even wear a mask to help erase Covid today. Whatever their reasons, especially if they believe they're healthy enough to come through the disease unscathed, their willingness to expose the more vulnerable is not a caring or loving action.

I have also seen women take strides forward in being accepted as equals. My mother had to give up her job as a secretary when she married. That's what women did in the 1930s. I'm also sure my father never changed a diaper. Since then, I've seen my granddaughters' husbands change diapers and support their working wives in every way they can. Actually, I've even seen my sons do this, and it brings both a smile to my face and hope for the future to my heart.

When I first went to work, I was still expected to do all the household chores, including taking care of all the needs of my five children, who ranged in age from two to eleven. And I fought, my entire career, for women's equal pay for equal work.

Now, instead of seeing things continue forward for women, I see us losing ground, including the right to be in charge of our own bodies. And my heart breaks listening to the news about all the rights being stripped from women in Afghanistan. I want those women, and all women, to stand up and shout against the injustice. But I also understand that the women in Afghanistan who do this will probably lose their lives. It's especially hard to imagine a silver lining for them.

And I know it will take more than just imagining for change to happen. Imagining may be a first step, after we no longer fear getting a disease that has the potential to kill us, but it needs to be followed by action, the work to actually make the changes that will make the world a better place. Silver linings seldom happen without someone clearing a path for them.

Yes, I cringe when thinking past Covid. Instead, I focus on the next small step forward. My silver lining is believing that each person has the ability to make such changes, and that lumped together these small actions, like speaking out at racial injustice or casting educated votes, will inch us forward day by day.

And at 82, that's as far forward as I'm willing to look. I want to remain a dreamer.

THERE IS NO GOING BACK

Pat Anthony

Trails burned now, crisscrossed
with fallen cedars brought down
by fire, grader, storm

so you pick a path well trodden
only by night animals: deer, loping coyote
follow it through sericea, switchgrass
and around second growth walls of sumac
to slip beneath a fence and take it all in

the tiny creek at your feet that knows
how to swell into unexpected torrent
the autumn beds of poison ivy twining
through brown brome escaped from hay fields
this massive cedar where you bury
your face in its drupes of blue berries

so much to look forward to beyond
soon snow-laden boughs to a spring
when once again narcissus and daffodil
will host a thousand resurrections
in the abandoned field where surely
a house once stood, fallen timbers

gone to rotted wood pulp now feeding
bulb and shoot, tight spikes that will
fill the camera lens, its bird's eye
of possibility but for now this very air
holds what will expand us breathing
in, out, in, out as we fuel dreams

new beams with which to construct bridges
leading us into new tomorrows
not by retracing our steps
down those disappeared trails
but by blazing new ones step by step
seasoned walking stick at the ready
and in our worn packs a fresh notebook where
we will pause along our new paths
to celebrate every little thing.

COVID AND THE CATERPILLAR

Thelma Zirkelbach

"In the light of the moon, a little bug lay on a leaf." So begins Eric Carle's *The Very Hungry Caterpillar,* one of my favorite books when I provided speech therapy for young children. When the sun comes up, the caterpillar eats one apple and one more piece of fruit each day, until the seventh day when he gorges on all sorts of food. Now a big caterpillar, he spins a cocoon and later emerges as a beautiful butterfly.

So what does this colorful book have to do with the pandemic and with me? Well, I did gorge on food, mainly ice cream, and I did live in a cocoon. All of us did. We wanted protection; but cocoons, for all the safety they provide, are dark and lonely places. In March 2020, the Houston rodeo closed down, and then it seemed the whole world shut down. Activities in my senior residence were cancelled, the dining room closed, and we were required to wear masks outside our apartments. Figuring out who was behind a mask was difficult. One lady asked if I was new here. After all, how could she tell? – we all have gray hair. Having meals delivered and eating alone in our apartments felt strange, but we were lucky in other ways. Unlike the caterpillar, we weren't completely alone. We could chat with neighbors in the mailroom or the garden. The building streamed "Hamilton" on our in-house channel. People became addicted to Zoom and even those who had eschewed Amazon shopped online. Yet I felt an undercurrent of sadness. I missed my old life, as memories of dining out, volunteer work, movie theaters and sports events receded into what seemed like the distant past.

These days, in July 2021, like the newborn butterfly, we are venturing into the world again, but it's harder than I expected. My new butterfly wings flutter timidly as I enter the Kroger store where I've shopped for years or go inside the bank instead of the drive-through. Now that the CDC has said that vaccinated people no longer have to wear masks, the outside world is confusing, even scary. President Biden said we reached a milestone, but it seems more like an obstacle to surmount. How do I know the person in the checkout line behind me at the supermarket is vaccinated? Does that building require masks or not? I keep a mask in the car just in case.

I have seen articles that say many people feel this way. It's normal. I am relieved that I'm normal as I wonder what to do with the basketful of masks I acquired – various colors to match my wardrobe. I'm weaning myself off ice cream and I plan to be ice cream free by the end of summer. I hope by then I can spread my wings with confidence as I float fully into the world.

UNMASKED

Rosemary Keevil

It was July 1st, which is Canada Day—sort of the equivalent to the US Independence Day. Here, in British Columbia, we were just entering into Phase Three of our COVID recovery plan. Did you hear me? That was PHASE THREE OF OUR COVID RECOVERY PLAN.

Do you know what that meant? It meant we could disrobe. Disrobe you say? Yes! Disrobe! Take off our masks!

It had been sixteen months—sixteen months that we had to wear masks to go out anywhere.

A quick peek at Wikipedia tells me that over the centuries, masks have been used for rituals, ceremonies, hunting, feasts, wars, theatre, fashion, sports, occupational, or protective purposes.

Ding, ding, ding! COVID masks are used for protective purposes.

I got so used to wearing those blankety-blank nuisances that part of me now misses them. I can't believe I am saying that. They were such a bother. There was a lot going on around my ears. Earrings: can't go out without earrings that match my outfit. Hearing aids: can't go out without my hearing aids—what is that you say, dearie? As an aside, it got very noisy around my ears as I fiddled with the two masks I wear. Yes, two: one fancy to match my outfit and underneath that, an ugly disposable one. I did this for two reasons: for extra protection, and so I could still wear lipstick while not soiling my fancy mask. Yes, I wore lipstick—sometimes you have to take your mask off to sip your Starbucks or perhaps breathe—what a concept! And I would not want to be seen without my matching lipstick. That is another story.

Speaking of matching, I put thought and energy into my outfits every day even though I didn't go very far, and I made sure that my masks complemented my clothes. I have some masks that are so fancy that I built an entire outfit around them—as one would do with a new pair of Jimmy Choo shoes. I have dozens of masks and some even have a scent like lavender.

Apparently, there is talk of COVID museums in the works. I am thinking of offering up my collection of masks.

MOVING AHEAD

Mary Jarvis

It seems that COVID has exacerbated and thrown into full view the cleavages and inequities in our society. We might have preferred to ignore those inequities, but they are there. Perhaps some of us knew more than we were consciously aware of. Being isolated and having serious divides about how to handle things only made matters worse.

As an individual, it seems there is little I can do to make a difference. But many individuals combining their efforts can perhaps add up to something significant. So what now?

I want to do what I can to improve my relationships with those of other races and ethnic groups. In my part of Texas – one of its most conservative areas – it seems that doing anything to make things better is frowned upon. But do I really care who frowns? Does it really make a difference in what I do? For lots of years that frowning would have made a difference in my actions. Maybe that's a blessing of the COVID time for me – finally refusing to let what others think deter me.

I want to learn new things. I'm retired from nearly fifty years as a librarian in a variety of library settings, in which I seemed to learn something new every day. It now takes more effort to learn new things. I know how to help people research and get accurate facts. I want to be giving back and to learn. Maybe I want to learn more about sustainable living on a personal scale – something I've thought about in the past but have done very little about. And this may become much more important as the climate is changing.

Since March 2020, when wearing a mask became one of our main precautions against COVID, I've tried to smile enough so that the smile reaches my eyes and the person with whom I'm talking can see that smile. I make sure to have a kind word for grocery store workers and others who have had to continue working, so that they might have at least one kind interaction each day. These two things I can – and will – continue to do going forward. I can only hope that others are trying to be kind as well.

Maybe if we each do something positive and encouraging each day, together we will make a difference.

MONA LISA REVIVED

Barbara Dee

Ann, your eyes are dark green. And brown.
Do they call that *hazel?* I asked you, mask-muffled.

I never noticed the mixture, the lighter flecks.
Before…

Before, your face only had one feature.
I only saw your lips, full and impossible to describe as a color.

Soft, light-brown primer and a pink topcoat painted
your lips that revealed so much—said and unsaid.

Before, my face had no mind of its own.
Your lips would stretch into even the slightest smile and mine would
    instantly follow suit.

Without your smile these last months,
without your smile to lead the way, mine gave up.

I only today realized all that your lips mean to me,
when I saw you in the coffee shop, both of us wearing no mask.

What would Mona Lisa be without her smile?
I pray we never know.

I will never take your beautiful smile for granted again.

BROKEN

Madeline Sharples

Since my husband died
I've been broken.
I know I give the impression
That I have it all together,
But that is just a white lie
I even tell myself.
I pretend I am strong
I pretend I am getting on
Without him. Yet,
I feel how empty life is
Now that he is gone.
People tell me
What a loving and caring man
He was and how lucky
I was to have him.
That's why I'm moving,
That's why I've taken on
This change so soon
Since he died.
I need to take
The daily reminders
The familiar routines away,
And begin to build new memories
Somewhere else.
Maybe then I can repair
The brokenness
And the loneliness
I'm feeling now.

AFTER GOODBYE

Sandra Carey Cody

How do you move on after you've said goodbye? How do you silence your doubts and stop asking yourself if you could have done more? Should you have asked another question? Or a different question? One that would have given more life to the person you loved? The person with whom you spent most of your life – almost sixty years, or, to be precise: fifty-nine years, five months, and thirteen days. Is that too much information? Maudlin? Probably. So, back to moving on.

It's not easy. My heart is raw. Everything feels wrong. It's tempting to blame Covid, but that's not fair. The thinking part of me knows I'm not part of an epic tragedy. What happened to me is the natural order of life, time demanding its due. Still, though Covid is not totally to blame, that nasty virus and its spawn, Delta, played a part. My Love started going downhill two (maybe three) years ago. We, or at least I, knew it was time to downsize, to get rid of the huge yard, an expanse where we'd hosted picnics, laughed with friends, and watched our sons chase fireflies. First, we hired someone to take care of the lawn, but it was still there and My Love, an independent person who'd always done everything himself, still worried about it, hated watching someone else do chores he considered his responsibility. So, we moved on.

We bought a townhouse. It was smaller, and responsibility for outside maintenance belonged to someone else. We started meeting our neighbors, adding to our circle of friends. Then Covid struck. With lightning speed, it seemed, though in hindsight, we had ample warning. If we had heeded the warnings, would it have been different? On a national and international level, probably, but that's another matter and far beyond my ken. On a personal level, I don't think anything would have made a difference. The isolation imposed by Covid and the downward spiraling of My Love's health came together and I am convinced the first accelerated the second, but even if it had not, change would have come. Even in the best of times, change is inevitable. We can't stop it, but we can choose how we react to it. Do we hide from it or do we meet it head-on? The answer seems obvious, but it comes with no instructions for how.

Into all this, as Covid slowly recedes (or not), add the reminders of another seemingly insurmountable occurrence – one that happened twenty years ago. Unlike Covid, which gave plenty of warning, the attacks on 9/11 were a shock, though perhaps not as different as it seems at first. The discontent that prompted the attacks was all around us if we'd only been paying attention. The pulse of history was throbbing across the planet. Most of us were at least dimly aware of the potential for explosion, but too busy living our lives to be overly concerned, confident that reason would find a way to avert an eruption. As we look back, horrified, yet proud that we survived, everywhere around us is the message: "We must never forget." How does this fit in? How do we move on and still honor the past?

I recently came across a quote by Albert Einstein: "We cannot solve our problems with the same level of thinking that created them." That makes sense, but again there are no instructions for how. What level of thinking can I use as a guide in my new reality? The only hint is that it must be different from my old level of thinking, the one I, like most women of my generation, learned at an early age: *two-by-two*.

How do I get past the *two-by-two* mindset? How do I learn to think solo? Again, the answer seems obvious. Call another solo to see a movie or have a meal in a restaurant. Maybe better, I'll venture into a theater or a restaurant alone. I can do that. I'll probably feel conspicuous, like everyone is looking at me, wondering why I'm alone, thinking there must be something wrong with me that I don't have friends. In reality, I doubt anyone will notice. Why should they? Everyone has their own life to live, their own insecurities to deal with. Yes, I can safely solo. That doesn't mean I must always be alone. I can seek out other solos. And not just solos. I can say *yes* to invitations from people who were part of the life I shared with My Love. I won't assume they're just being nice. I'll believe they really want to spend time with me, the individual, not just the leftover half of a *two-by-two*.

There are countless opportunities to explore things I didn't have time for when I was half of a *two-by-two*. It's time to look beyond old boundaries. Am I too old to learn a new language? It's time to find out. What if I am? What if I fail? Does it matter? If I don't master the language, I'm sure to learn at least a few words, and I'll be richer for them. So, failure, at least complete failure, isn't likely. And, if the unlikely happens, there's always another option. Cooking, for example. I've never been an adventurous cook. Maybe it's time to change that. I can invite friends over for dinner and try something new. What's the worst that can happen? My experiment might be a flop, totally inedible. What will I do then? I'll laugh and open a can of soup. My friends won't love me less because of it. They might actually like me better because I tried and failed. No, not failed. Imperfection is not failure. Imperfection is human; it is inherent in change, an inescapable part of moving on, the one thing all humans have in common.

I've rambled a lot to come to a simple realization. Change has been an integral part of everyone's life during the past year-and-a-half. We move on by adopting a new way of thinking. That takes courage. Not the huge *win-a-medal* kind of courage, but courage in small things, like laying bare the insecurities we try to hide, exposing the scars from the searing losses we've experienced.

Illuminate the hidden places of our souls. Honor them.

Back to my original question: What's after goodbye? Some new hellos.

STITCH BY STITCH

Erin Philbin

It is day number "Who the hell knows?" of the pandemic. It feels as though the rest of the world is isolating, but I have been working full-time as a speech language pathologist at a skilled nursing facility. While the obsession of keeping Covid from my patients and loved ones possesses me, a new worry has begun to worm its way into my consciousness: perhaps I am simply not doing lockdown correctly.

I hear people reporting that they are exercising more, using their time to kickstart a new fitness program. Pounds are being lost, and clothing sizes are dropping. Even people's pets are losing weight. This is a wonderful plan. My first day out walking, I manage to trip over an infinitesimal crack in a sidewalk. My bruised face, knees, hands, and pride keep me from returning to my exercise plan. Besides, it was cutting into my snacking time.

People say they are using their time to clean out their homes, getting a fresh start on their lives. What a great idea! Since I am a hoarder at heart, I can only imagine what a fresh start would look like. Knowing how much easier it is to deal with someone else's crap, I decide to start on my daughter's room. She has recently moved into her own apartment, so we will not get into each other's way. I uncover years' worth of papers, school projects, books, art supplies, and memories. I manage to drag everything into my room for some clear decisions, before I bore myself out of my mind and abandon the whole plan.

Everywhere, there is discussion of something called "sourdough starter." After some research, I decide to save the time and simply buy a loaf of bread.

I try writing, but there is no energy for the lighthearted stories I love to share. Despair threatens to overwhelm me. I focus on providing care during the day and have nothing left by evening.

I decide it might be a good time, once again, to learn to knit. After all, I've crocheted since I was a young girl, and really, how different can it be? Three hours later, I remember how different it can be. While I am burying the evidence in the bottom of a large plastic storage container, I find The Lady.

The Lady is how I have always referred to a hand-painted needlepoint canvas that my mother-in-law, Sally, surprised me with after she taught me how to stitch over two decades ago. It is of a woman from the 1920s, dressed for an evening out in an elegant gown and coat with fur collar, looking out a gilt-edged window at a winter evening sky. Sally had also given me all the threads necessary to complete the project. Not just the cotton threads I could afford, but also, amazing wools, silks, and metallics that I had only dreamed of using.

I have spent many hours stitching The Lady with Sally as we share our lives. She tells me of growing up in the Depression, of being a military wife through World War II, Korea, and Vietnam. There are stories of families, and friendships found and lost, of difficulties and experiences, of always living on a new base, moving across the country, and sometimes to another country. They are stories of hardship, but more often of humor and adventure and of women getting up and starting over, making connections again and again. When Sally passes away, I put away the unfinished needlepoint. A part of me feels that by completing it, I will lose all those happy memories. I will be closing a chapter I am not ready to finish.

It's been years since I have worked on The Lady; now I make the first few tentative stitches. Within moments, I am smiling. I had forgotten how much I loved this. My stitching becomes a meditation, my racing heart slows, and my mind clears, as the rhythm of my hands forms the stitches. Working on The Lady becomes respite as summer passes into fall and winter. Her lovely background of warm yellows keeps the darkness at bay. For the first time in a very long time, I find myself taking joy in the journey of my craft. Stitch by stich, I breathe life into the piece, and take back some of the joy that the project has given me. Once the background is completed, I move to wispy gray clouds reflected through the window. I then stitch her hat with a feather plume and her voluminous gray coat. Although I worried forever about stitching The Lady's face, when it is completed, we both have small, contented smiles.

When the project is finished, there is no sadness, only joy and remembrance of love and shared memories. I don't hesitate to take her to the framers. The next day I head to a local needlepoint shop that I have passed many times but never entered. When I open the door, I am overwhelmed by the beauty of hundreds of awaiting canvases, a riot of color and texture from thousands of threads and generous women waiting to welcome me.

I choose a small picture of a city scene at night, and rich, joyful colors to stitch it. While the world hesitantly begins to reopen, already there is talk of a variant strain of Covid gathering like storm clouds. I gather my canvas and threads, sit in my favorite chair, and stitch.

Hoping

LEANING INTO TOMORROW WITH IMPASSIONED HOPE

Debra Thomas

As I look to a future beyond COVID, I am filled with hope. Not a naïve hope, based on blind optimism, but a determined hope that persisted despite distance and division. Not a stubborn persistence, for even the strongest wills faltered during these trying times. Mine is a hope that rose from the ashes of pandemic deaths, police brutality, and heartless family separations at the border, and then, as I watched individuals come together—armed with empathy and driven by heartfelt purpose—my hope transformed into a brighter, unwavering, impassioned hope.

Looking back on the stunning events that unfolded as the coronavirus swept across the globe, I still find myself in disbelief. How fortunate for those who survived. How tragic for those who passed away or lost dear ones. For many of us—locked down and separated from those we love—our lives slowed down. Sitting in our homes, we embarked on unexpected journeys, looking outward through television and social media and turning inward as we reflected on our own life choices.

What exactly did we learn? And what do we carry with us into the future?

We watched as the number of coronavirus deaths soared nightly. We heard accounts of nurses holding iPads so dying patients could say goodbye to their families. We saw refrigerated trucks brought in to store bodies as morgues filled beyond capacity. Some experienced this nightmare in their own lives. Others were spared the virus' direct invasion. But the pandemic still affected livelihoods, canceled weddings and proms, and kept families and friends apart for indefinite periods of time.

We all grieved. We all felt helpless. We all wanted to do something—anything—to help.

My own heavy heart began to lighten as I saw communities rally: applauding essential workers, establishing GoFundMe accounts for families who'd lost loved ones, and creating phone banks to check on elderly neighbors. Even the least tech savvy among us became Zoom experts as family and friends reached out through cyberspace to stay connected. Phone calls. FaceTime. Text messaging. Emails. We found ways to communicate with each other despite the distance, bringing joy, comfort, and companionship during this time of isolation. Even schools and businesses kept as much forward movement as possible through virtual means.

Together, we learned how to carry on.

During this time, we also witnessed heart-wrenching racial and social injustice. Between breaking news of COVID surges, we watched the chilling video of George Floyd's murder, which exemplified and exposed the frequent injustices suffered by people of color at the hands of those meant to protect them. At the same time, we continued to hear reports of desperate asylum seekers fleeing unspeakable violence in their countries in hopes of finding safe haven in the U.S.—only to be turned away or held indefinitely at our border. News of family separations persisted as well, with hundreds of migrant children still lost in the heartless bureaucracy that yanked them from their parents' arms. Dark clouds of hatred, fear, and anger seemed to obscure any traces of hope.

Then, in the darkness, flashes of light emerged.

Black Lives Matter movements began across our nation, joined by people of all colors, ages, and walks of life—an inspiring sign of communion at a time of great division. In response to the suffering at the border, inter-faith groups, such as Interfaith-RISE in New Jersey and Interfaith Community for Detained Immigrants in Chicago, brought people of diverse religions together to help those in detention centers in the U.S. and those living in horrendous conditions at migrant shelters on the Mexican side of our border. Immigrant rights organizations, like Border Angels in San Diego and No More Deaths in Tucson, continued their outreach despite COVID. Determined to carry on their humanitarian aid, masked volunteers still provided food and necessities at overcrowded migrant shelters, while groups of volunteers hiked to strategic places in the desert, leaving water to prevent migrant deaths by dehydration. 'Love has no borders' is their motto. Amidst the deep sadness of the time, these acts of empathy and common goodness lifted my spirits and restored my faith in humanity—a response experienced by many.

As I now reflect on these moments in our recent history, I see how essential it is that we carry those images with us into the future. All of them. The nurse holding the iPad. George Floyd calling for his mother. The wide-eyed toddler looking up at the Border Patrol agent moments before she is taken from her mother. With those painful images, we must also remember those that gave us hope: the thousands of paper hearts placed in windows throughout the U.S. to "spread the love;" the shouts and cheers at 7 p.m. in N.Y.C. in support of essential workers; the throngs of peaceful, masked Black Lives Matter marchers in countless cities across the country; and finally, the aid workers, still at our borders, bringing food and comfort to those with nowhere else to go.

If we do this, we will never forget *why* they came together, and we will always remember that they were united by a higher purpose.

This is where all hope for our future lies.

Take what we've learned. Carry it forward. Do what we can, in whatever ways we can. For some, it may be as simple as helping an elderly neighbor or as involved as becoming a leader in a social justice organization. For me, it's writing about injustice to raise awareness and rouse empathy. If we've learned anything during this life-changing time of COVID, it's the importance of staying informed and aware—and then taking action. Thoughts without actions allow both pandemics and injustice to persist. We are all responsible. We are all capable. If we act together, our collective strength can lead to positive change in the world.

This is how I want to lean into the post-COVID future. Not as an *I*, but as a *we*. Enough of words mumbled through masks of isolation and ignorance. It's time to speak to each other clearly of truth. Enough talk about walls, borders, and barriers. Now is the time to build doorways, hallways, and bridges that bring us together. Enough separation and fear. It's time to look to the future as a *we,* connected by the grit, grace, and courage that got us through this difficult time and united by our common goal of a kinder, safer world. This is how I want to step into our future—together—with impassioned hope.

MUSINGS ON COMMUNITY HEALTH CARE

Claire McCabe

It's a Saturday afternoon in August 2021, and my usual drive through COVID-19 testing centers are either operating on limited schedules, or completely closed. Since vaccinations came out in the spring, there seems less of a need for testing. But I need to find a place. Today. I just got word that a friend came down with COVID, two days after we both attended an outdoor picnic. We're both vaccinated, yet no one's completely safe. I will be back teaching in-person in less than two weeks and need to be clear of COVID.

In the six days it takes for the picnic committee to notify me, I have been in contact with lots of people. Mostly masked. But sometimes not – for example, two hours unmasked next to my eighty-six-year-old book club friend. I love Pat's comments on whatever we read, and I appreciate that she practices a Buddhist stillness. I see compassion in her kind eyes, and I don't want that light to go out. I'm hungry to hear more of her opinions and stories.

When I exhaust my usual testing sights, I dive deeper on the internet: nothing is available for two days out. I poke into some municipal websites and finally discover a pop-up testing site, still open for another hour. And it accepts walk-ups.

My GPS takes me into a paved lot between a city park and a rundown townhouse complex. Brightly colored ride-on toys litter some of the front yards. In another yard, white wire wickets surround a statue of the Blessed Virgin, side-dressed with faded plastic flowers. I notice a young mother pushing a stroller, and a man who walks a muscled mixed-breed dog wearing a chain collar. I like this neighborhood; it's full of young life that reminds me of my own former life.

I lived in a similar complex as a graduate student. There were a few other students, but most of my neighbors then were hardworking people with children. Some, like me, were on welfare. As a single mother raising a child and finishing my own education, I didn't have much money. But I had a future. I took my child to public clinics, and thanked the nurses who worked there day in, day out, caring for the many different faces of those hopeful families.

I exit my car and see a van that looks like a double-sized ice cream truck with two windows, each staffed by a health care professional.

The families ahead of me have children that are too young for COVID vaccines and need negative tests so the children can return to in-person schooling. At the front of one line is a mother with two daughters, their hair tied up in ponytails against the August heat. They are done quickly. At the front of the second line, where I wait, is a tall, dark-haired man with a son young enough to still hold his father's hand.

The nurse slides open her window and hands the father a clear plastic packet that contains a sterile swab and a receiving tube. I watch as she explains and gestures to the father about how to swab the inside of his son's nose. The father pulls down his son's mask and inserts the swab in a nostril; the boy rises on his tiptoes and leans away, but doesn't cry. It's over quickly.

And then it's my turn. The procedure is painless, and at this point in the pandemic, routine. I'll have results in forty-eight hours. I get back in my car and drive slowly out of the neighborhood. I make the sign of the cross as I pass the Blessed Virgin. I ask that she keep all of the families here safe, that she keep me safe, and if she has any clout, that she please see that this pandemic is over just as quickly as the swab tests.

FREEDOM

Charlotte Phillips

In my dreams, my thoughts and movements are COVID-free. I drive to the office to meet with colleagues and stop at the store on the way home. I don't think about masks, or hand sanitizer, or how long I will need to wait to visit at-risk family if I interact with people outside the bubble.

In my dreams, I gleefully accept invitations—weddings, birthday parties, children's recitals, school plays, and ball games, movies, and lunches. I don't think about the size of the crowd, how long I can stand to wear a mask, or whether proof of vaccine is required for participation.

In dreamland, I visit sick friends and do what I can to lift their spirits. I do this in person, not via videoconference. I hold hands, dispense hugs, and make tea.

Then I wake up and face the reality of another variant, another surge, another week of thousands of unnecessary deaths. I check my mask and hand-sanitizer supply. I check my schedule to see where I can get a fourteen-day stretch of zero exposure so I can visit at-risk family members. I take calls from friends, colleagues, and family members desperate for human connection. I do what I can. I walk in my yard for relief and to daydream of a different reality and to remind myself that dreams can come true. With most of the world working overtime on a common vision of a COVID-free world, this dream has a real chance.

FLY

Ariela Zucker

"Also he sent forth a dove from him, to see if the waters were abated from off the face of the ground"
— GENESIS 8:8, KING JAMES BIBLE

It's been over a year, he says to the dove,
as the ark rocks violently then comes to a halt.
And he opens the hatch and charges – Fly!
Small against the dark ark, a white dove,
hardly visible in a world that turned stark,
above the flooded creation, searching for a sign.

To see if the waters were abated from off the face of the ground,
it flies. Over land that lost its lines, over rimless oceans,
along rivers forming new trails. Under the heavy blanket of stillness,
now that the rains subside.

Forty days since the water settled, hope can widen its expanse.
A dove carrying a plucked olive leaf, and a rainbow piercing the clouds.
A promise for a world to regain its lines, with rivers recovering their
    paths
to oceans once again within their edgings.

It's been over a year…

SONGBIRDS OF LIFE

Dorothy Preston

I feel as though I've crawled out of a dark cave.

After over a year of COVID, I was raw and angry at the world and felt isolated and alone.

Self-cordoned from empathetic comments on social media, I walled myself in.

My creative spark was nonexistent—like lighting a match in a windy rainstorm. Nothing. A solid year of nothing.

And although the world is still in turmoil, suddenly I feel like a bear emerging from hibernation after a long cold winter into the lush green grass that abounds his lair.

Everything is suddenly shiny and beautiful.

I am inspired to write with every turn of my head, every songbird that sings, every hummingbird that flutters by my window—its singular innocence and beauty singing to my soul.

Nature never stops. Nature doesn't care about what we humans are distracted by or angry about.

It just keeps thrumming, beat by beat, flutter by flutter, to the vibration of the universe with neither a care nor thought for what anyone else thinks.

I want to emulate the songbirds' simplicity, their ease of existence.

If only we humans could.

What a peaceful and beautiful world this could be if we all soared through life without a care.

Oh, lovely Songbird, occupy my soul and fill me with your love.

SERENDIPITY

Jo-Ann Vega

A year has passed and they are still visiting.

The visits, always irregular and with different combinations of the original group of young teenagers, began in the summer of 2020, as the pandemic was in its most terrifying stage. One brutally hot July afternoon I happened to look outside my home window and noticed half-a-dozen girls, along with several younger children, basking under the expansive arms of my neighbor's willow tree.

I'd scarcely seen a dozen people in the neighborhood in the months since the state was shut down. I was lonely and curious. How were young people, our future, experiencing the pandemic? An educator with thirty years of experience, I've been tracking changing demographics nearly as long. The preliminary findings of enforced social isolation on mental health are sobering.

On weekly excursions for food, I'd been struck by the harsh judgment and watchful scrutiny of others, a palpable fear directed at all others, who could bring contagion and near-certain death. Were you wearing a mask properly, sneezing or coughing, walking in the prescribed direction down the aisle, maintaining social distance, avoiding eye contact and idle chatter? The usual din of the grocery store was replaced with the sounds of shoppers scurrying to return to the safety of their personal bunkers, and workers silently performing their jobs. I missed greetings and idle chatter with familiar faces.

I decided to go outside. Having had sales and counseling experience, I've generally found that if you express genuine interest in others and treat them with respect, they will respond. As I walked towards the group, I didn't want to startle them, so I called out to announce myself. "It's an amazing experience, isn't it? Don't you almost feel hugged by the tree?"

The group turned towards the sound of my voice and to each other as they nodded. I asked how they were, talked about the tree, and then got around to the pandemic. "How are you coping with the pandemic?"

The teenagers all looked down. One said, "I'm scared."

I looked directly at the group as I spoke. "Yes, it's scary. Are you and every one you know okay?"

The answer: "Yes."

Without much prompting, they started talking. They hated Zoom; their grades were suffering; the teachers weren't giving them the attention they needed; and they missed the experience of school and being with their peers, with something to do. They were spending too much time alone and filling it themselves. They wanted to spend more time with their parents.

I told them some version of: *I feel really bad for you. This is such an important time in your lives. Try to make the best of it. Avoid putting yourselves in risky situations and above all, respect yourselves as budding women.* I encouraged them to talk with their parents and share their concerns. After a quarter hour or so, they said they had to go back home, and lived in the neighborhood. I thanked them for talking and we went our separate ways.

To my surprise, several continued to make unannounced visits, and stayed until prompted by me to leave. The doorbell would ring; I'd answer and step outside to talk with the girls. Sometimes I saw them twice a week, then weeks would pass before they would return.

I asked the obvious questions. Why do you keep coming back? What is it about me? I'm old enough to be your grandmother. I talk fast, move around, ask questions, and tell stories. Do you like me?

Their answers: Yes. You talk to us. You're interested in us. My grandmother is nothing like you. She doesn't speak with me the way you do.

I appreciated their honesty and replied: "No one gets past fifty years old without learning a few things, and yes, surviving a few bad decisions. Trust your family more. Adults don't always know how to talk to you either. They would love to hear from you."

After several visits, the girls tried to secure my endorsement for their plan to use the neighborhood boys for their own amusement, to relieve their boredom. I told them I could not support them. The behavior wasn't appropriate. I didn't want to be a part of it. I'd been encouraging them to get beyond the quick retort, to consider consequences, good and bad, to choose their answer instead of reacting, blah, blah, blah, adult stuff they didn't want to hear.

One of them, on a fast track to adulthood, clearly expecting a different answer, snapped at me, "Why not?!" and stood erect, as if bracing for an argument.

I faced her and in a level voice asked, "Do you speak to your grandmother this way?"

Her defiant answer, "Yes. I talk this way in my house!"

Without missing a beat, I replied, "I always speak to and treat you with respect. I expect you to do the same."

I could feel their impatience as I briefly explained that I am a teacher, an elder, not their friend or parent, and reassured them before announcing my decision. "I like you and want you to think about what I said. Do not come back until you can treat me with respect."

I paused. "If that means I don't see you again, I'm okay with that." In silence we parted.

Weeks passed without a visit. Then the doorbell rang. I was surprised and pleased to find familiar faces. Without my characteristic exuberance, I greeted them as I stepped onto the front entrance.

"Hello. You came back."

After some brief bantering I asked, "Were you angry at me after you left?"

"No."

I looked at them. "Why?"

"You were right."

They continued to make unannounced visits. Our discussions became more interactive. When I asked the ever-faithful visitor her opinion about something, she offered her reply with her characteristic quiet assurance. "I'm going to wait until I know more."

Her answer was amazing! I emphatically shouted. "Wow! Sometimes you say things that surprise me in a very good way." A slight pause followed by, "This did!"

She beamed. We chatted some more, I babbled, and then teenagers being teenagers with no conception of time, I moved towards the front steps and informed them it was time to leave. Dinner was awaiting me.

Here's what I'm learning about youth who will graduate from high school in three to four years. It's not a representative sample but the research backs them up.

Their opinion on school and Zoom never changed.

They want to be around adults and are seeking guidance. Why else would they keep coming back to visit the old lady with white hair who tries to connect with them? They've lost a valuable year that will reverberate throughout their lives. They recognize the future looks scary. I sense they have decidedly mixed feelings and dread about the future, their futures, our futures.

Let's lean into them. We need each other.

LEANING INTO TOMORROW

Lin M. Brummels

I look back at yesterday,
start to fall,
just in time catch hold
of a bit of moonlight
revealing the rocky path
traveled in times past
when escaping
what I believed to be
a broken family.

My post-WWII parents
lost hope in their future;
too many kids to feed,
rented farm ground,
borrowed money.

They were no doubt like
many poor farm families
trying to scratch a living
in sandy soil
that should have been left
as native grass
in the great Sandhills.

Leaning into tomorrow
I regain balance,
stumble along
a path toward sunrise;
see wind towers
sprouting from ground
that used to grow crops.

Even on foggy days
when the way is murky,
like today,
I embrace the future,
know sun will shine
on my imperfect
but lovely family.

LEANING TOWARD HAPPINESS, MAYBE PLEASURE

Marlene Samuels

As difficult as it's been for me to admit to anyone, including my closest family members, the pandemic actually offered me a surprising array of personal growth opportunities. They included an increased level of introspection—the kind I never made time for during the pre-

Covid era owing to far too many daily distractions. Better yet, I faced extra time during quarantine in which to assess things in my life that truly merit my attention, and in the category of "things," I probably added several individuals who've been easier to let go of than I might ever have imagined.

My newly empowered self stemmed from one irrefutable cause, or was it an excuse? I was encouraged by very limited, often nonexistent, opportunities to interact with friends and family or to engage in activities away from what had become my cave. In professional psychiatric circles, our months of Covid-driven isolation and altered lifestyles might have been referred to as a "mid-course correctional."

Those surprising benefits that rewarded me with new happiness and pleasure, unexpected as they've been, are beginning to lose their endurance power now. My new concern: will we ever go back to "the way it was before?" What if, instead, we're doomed to ride the fluctuating tides of various mutating Covid strains? Yet, on my upbeat days, I look toward a not-too-distant and optimistic future. It is in that place where we will see this powerful global plague leveling out much in the way the notorious flu pandemic of 1918 did. After all, don't most of us currently receive annual flu vaccines—the long-lived virus of constantly mutating form whose vaccines keep pace? Again, I temper my inclination to worry. Instead, I hope optimistically that we'll continue learning and evolving in our Covid-management skills.

"What gives you pleasure? What makes you happy?" the announcer asks. I'm listening to the podcast entitled *The Daily Stoic*, one of my newly found "courtesy of Covid" interests. Saturday's *Daily Stoic* is twice as long and challenging. Today is Saturday. I consider my possible answers seriously as I search for one of great philosophical significance. The first ones that come to me are the constants in my Covid-controlled life because I realize how much of my increased happiness and pleasure is due to my gigantic Rhodesian Ridgebacks, George and Ted.

Throughout this past year-and-a-half, we've spent most of our hours and days together—an amazing, unanticipated privilege for me. I've basked in their unconditional love, nonjudgmental affection, and unparalleled loyalty. Before our pandemic months, I had no ability to envision that their constant companionship—enhanced by their extrasensory perceptions of my low and high moods—could deliver such benefits.

During the first century A.D., the Greek philosopher Epictetus asked the same two questions about happiness and pleasure as did the podcaster. Epictetus even wrote a book he intended to be a manual for how to gain mental freedom and happiness in every circumstance. What might he have suggested if he were among us today experiencing Covid and looking ahead to post-Covid times?

Had I given any serious thought to such questions before our pandemic-altered state of life? Most likely not. Was I having difficulty coming up with a clear response to the podcaster's question or did I simply not know? At once I realized that every source of my happiness and pleasure—likely true for most of us—has been in a constant state of flux. They've been evolving in the same way our minds, bodies, and personalities have, except that these past months of Covid have encouraged me to delve more deeply.

Now, I lean into a new period of what I hope is one of vastly diminished constraints. Unlike the humans in my life—children, spouse, relatives, friends—my two constant canine companions don't hold my comments about political events against me. They neither care nor worry about Covid. Consequently, I regard them with a fair degree of envy, as I realize my anxiety about what's to come increases daily.

Besides my canines, what and who gives me pleasure, especially in our uncertain, plague-affected times? Are they material items, living beings, interesting experiences, even sensory ones? I've thought about dark chocolate that I enjoyed in Paris, and dream of rich homemade coffee ice cream I ate sitting on an uncomfortable metal chair watching the River Seine. But that begets a different worry: will there ever again be a time when I will find myself enjoying ice cream while sitting along the Seine?

Still, I continue to look toward the future with hopefulness. Surely, somewhere out on the distant horizon, are those attainable "things" that will provide me pleasure and enduring happiness. While writing this essay, it's become evident that our collective hopes are for a "leveling out" of our modern plague to a point that will allow for a return to pre-Covid life.

My sons, adaptable young men who've worked from home, have taken these past months in stride. They've evolved into impressive chefs and enthusiastic readers, and also have excelled at incorporating Zoom into their daily lives. It's a skill—cum habit—they've shared with me, and they are now committed to maintaining Zoom contacts "post-

Covid" as a means of keeping in touch with distant family members and faraway friends.

All is not gloom and doom in the current, most likely forever-altered state of our pandemic world, as I've learned. What keeps me optimistic and has given me pleasure are the numerous opportunities I've taken advantage of during the Covid months. The activities, living beings, places and culture I've found rewarding and pleasurable, have been virtual. But again, I revisit my focus upon the Stoics as one avenue I'll follow as we approach a post-Covid or more likely a less-Covid-dominated lifestyle.

Who have I missed, and with whom have I strived to communicate most? New habits developed at the height of our quarantine and Covid-induced constraints will persist. I'm pleased, even happy, to notice how prolific and consistent my writing has been during these months. And all the while, I maintained my connections with a group of women writing colleagues, both activities that led to happy feelings about my increasing creativity but especially to a more positive view about humanity's future.

I've found my way back to my kitchen, but as a braver, more self-confident version of my culinary self. I have been transformed into an experimental scientist, who realizes she's much less concerned about others' food likes and dislikes. "Get over it!" I think as I cook and create. "Grow up, eat up, and stop picking at your food," while my favorite music—old and new—plays in my ear-buds to sooth and excite me. George and Ted, my constants, help maintain order on the kitchen floor whenever necessary.

Nature offers me pleasure and happiness on the long walks I'd always been too busy to take advantage of "before." I now understand precisely what it was that all those famous "walkers" derived from all their meanderings, rural and urban. I felt compelled to reread some of those walkers' notes: Muir and Wordsworth, Woolf and Kierkegaard, Dickens and Thoreau: "Walking through nature was a kind of pilgrimage without a destination." I returned to Aristotle whose writing I first investigated for thoughts about happiness and pleasure, looking for inspiration about gaining emotional stamina to survive stressful events. Aristotle also was a great walker and focusing on all those walkers fueled my happiness for the ability, despite our pandemic, to develop a walking practice.

I remind myself that Epictetus, my newly discovered Covid-era hero, believed happiness to be the highest attainable good, that misery results from our inability to differentiate between what we can and cannot control. Am I practicing? Understanding that I can't control the state of this plague, nor the conduct of others in its midst, has served me well.

When I consider what's to come, while keeping those wise words front and center in my mind, my responsibilities will rest upon managing my personal conduct. To be of a positive state of mind and of a positive influence constitute my hopes for a significantly less Covid-controlled future.

FACING EAST

Sandra Stanko

Trees green, swaying.
Water opaque, flowing.
Forest shady, encompassing
Eastern white pine
Black oak
Poison ivy – *Toxicodendron radicans.*
Complexity within the commonness.
All present in the present, a patterned balance.
No worries here.
No ruminations or projections.
The Pennsylvania sun shines right at this moment,
Sealing the meaning in its heat, light, sparkle — hope.
All is well.
All is well.
All is well.

WONDER

Allison Allen

In the Chinese language, the word for 'crisis' is said to be composed of two characters, one representing danger and the other, opportunity. We have been in crisis for too long.

———

Breathing shallow, back tight, mind agitated. Telltale signs of heightened anxiety and stress have reappeared, familiar if unwanted companions this past year-and-a-half. After the cautious hopefulness of 2021's late spring and early summer, the tender shoots of my optimism are wilting under hot rays and surging temperatures in this Indian Summer of politics, pandemics, polarization and personal dilemmas.

It's as though we have failed a test somehow. As though the Universe, losing patience, having tried and failed to catch our attention with a quiet word, then a gentle touch, then a firm tap on our shoulder, finally an iron hand grasping our arm, is resorting to a grand piano dropped from the third story on top of our heads.

I can't shake this feeling that the Universe is demanding something from us. And we're not listening.

———

Our culture has great faith we can 'fix' almost anything – people, pandemics and problems.

"How to Fix Politics – Bold Solutions to America's Problems" trumpets the clickbait headline. If only, I think. "Seven Ways to Fix The Pandemic – And Stop The Next One" another reads. Really? There is even a Fixer Mentality. The Google search tells me it's a person who must try to fix anything they perceive as defective, hurt, or lacking in happiness.

Leaky toilets, broken washing machines, a car that won't start, a broken arm, or a computer that won't connect to my printer. Those things, and a gazillion others like them, are easy fixes.

Pandemics, politics, poverty, dysfunctional organizations, the -isms, climate change, relationship problems, our healthcare system? Infinite moving parts, connections we don't see or understand, interdependencies invisible to us, individuals' behavior, systemic issues, our beliefs and values…all play a part, and managing or changing the whole is unimaginably complex. These are not leaky toilets.

And I worry because we treat each other as if they were. There is one right way of seeing it, my way, my tribe's way. And we criticize, label, blame, moralize about those who don't see it like that. We weaponize facts, gang up, unfriend, and fear.

In 2020, year 1 A.H. (Annus Horribilis), I strained, always trying to bridge the gaps. Ferreting out facts in search of the one that would change minds. Spending too much time and mental energy mediating, wrestling with my own lesser angels and others'. In search of The Truth, surely it was there? Often dismayed at myself, my friends, family.

A great need to be certain in a time of great uncertainty. Perhaps therein lies our danger.

I wonder.

———

I have learned a thing. When I have been pushing mightily, with great heat and insistent energy to change something or someone, and change is not happening, it's time to stop and get thoughtful. What is it I'm not listening to?

———

My sister and I are talking over our latest family dilemma involving our brother. Is it the 40th time? The 100th? We've long since lost count. Equal parts poor judgment, lovability, and a tangled web of deficits and issues we cannot unravel, here we are again, covering well-traveled territory. He should do this, we should say that, maybe if he (fill in the blank).

"Sometimes I wonder," sis says slowly, thoughtfully, "what would happen if we just stopped trying to fix him. If we started from, this is him, we love him, he may not change the way we want."

I wonder, not for the first time, when my baby sister became so wise. We 'know' what steps would change his life for the better; we have many brilliant action plans that assume he changes.

But what would the plan be if we assume a reality where little changes, the situation persists despite our sage plans? How would our questions change? What would we do differently? How would WE have to change?

I wonder.

———

2021, year 2 A.H., my need to be certain is becoming as heavy on my heart as Marley's chain. Can I lay it down?

———

I peruse the comments from readers in my national newspaper most mornings. In 2020, I often despaired of humans, myself included, and truth be told, still do at times in 2021. I, more than my fair share, righteously want to SET PEOPLE STRAIGHT.

In 2021, I resolved to make a practice of asking myself, when I am tempted to comment or retort, does anyone need to know what I think? Am I adding anything useful? Will this change a mind, or a heart? Am I acting from a loving or a critical spirit? Sometimes I succeed in this; just lately I have been less successful. Ebb and flow. Still, I remain committed to this practice.

There is a glimmer of a shift I observe in myself though. From my discouragement and irritation, often now I can hear a note in the discord I didn't notice before. All are confused, bewildered, overwhelmed, and just trying to make sense of the profound disorder around us as best we can. I soften.

Stressed humans are rarely at their best, though they are nearly always doing their best.

———

Einstein famously observed, "The world as we have created it is a product of our thinking. It cannot be changed without changing our thinking."

What if the magnitude of disorder around us is simply the reflection of disordered thinking in all of us? What if we stopped, got thoughtful, and began to ask different questions? What if instead of trying to change people, we listened to them? How would WE have to change then? What would we create then?

What if therein lies our opportunity?

I wonder.

Standing outside under the moonless heavens, I strain to see all the points of light I know are there. A favorite pastime when we visit the ranch is to lie in the bed of our pickup with binoculars in hand. I must be patient to allow time for eyes to adjust. Pointing my glasses at the Milky Way, I catch my breath at the limitless multitude of stars there are, the depth and breadth of their numbers. Binoculars are best for this. Telescopes are too precise, too narrow, too laser-focused on detail to fully appreciate what is before me. Even with binoculars, I find if I shift my perspective to use my soft peripheral vision, if I look obliquely, I comprehend more deeply the vast expanse in all its spangled majesty.

I see more, I see differently.

OFF THE CUFF

Jeanne Baker Guy

I would tell you
I haven't been
Affected
At all
By the forever-and-ever
Pandemic
But
Sleep does not provide rest
And I'm too exhausted
To talk to you

I'm listening instead

Poet David Whyte's counsel
Offers a path I can lean into:
Risk yourself to be here now
During this time of
Incredible unknowing

And so I shall

The storm of life
Doesn't need to capsize my heart
There is joy deep inside me
Let me search there
For the rest I need

A DIFFERENT KIND OF HUG

Jo Virgil

When we pay attention, life always has lessons for us, even when things happen that we didn't wish for. Did anyone wish for COVID? I suspect not. But the isolation, the tragic illnesses and deaths, the tamping down of social interactions—all of those things are, if we listen with our hearts, messages of how our culture will be affected and what our future may become. And what our future becomes depends on how we choose to respond.

When I think of what our lives will be like once we get past the pandemic, the first thing that comes to my mind is learning to feel gratitude. So many things we have taken for granted have been shelved for well over a year. Now that we enter into the next episode of human existence, I keep thinking of the Stoicism philosophy quote: "The obstacle is the way." COVID has certainly been an obstacle, and while we have had to deal with stress, loneliness, and in some cases serious illness or even the death of a loved one, we do have the option to use our curiosity to tap into the lesson that exists in this obstacle.

Especially in our western world, we have lived mostly comfortably for the past many years, but so much so that we've taken it all for granted a bit—things like meeting up with friends and family for visits, attending conferences and discussion groups, traveling anywhere we want, even going to the grocery store for our favorite foods. Even now that about half of the people in the U.S. have gotten vaccines, we still have to pay attention to the variants and be cautious, mostly having to avoid social interaction. So when we get to the point where we are beyond the threat of COVID, won't we all have a deeper appreciation for hugs, for sharing laughter, for meeting new friends, for feeling safe to explore nearby and far away?

One thing I have taken from the COVID days, and that I will take with me far into the future, is the gift of learning from children. My two granddaughters, ages seven and ten, simply did their best to adapt, and in the few times I was able to be with them, I came to realize the importance of being flexible. Before the vaccination was available, we didn't hug, but we pretended to do virtual hugs, and that always made them laugh. When we visited, we did so outside, and the joy and energy the kids showed reminded me to just enjoy this moment.

I realized again the importance of accepting change when recently I was leaving to go home from a visit to my grandkids. Amelia, the seven-year-old, said, "Grandmommy, I know we aren't supposed to hug, but I have an idea." I had no clue what she meant, but she turned her back toward me, slowly stepped backwards coming over to me, and when she got close, she put her arms behind her and wrapped them around me for a Backwards Hug. Wow! Did that feel good—and safe!

COVID can teach us to adapt. It has been an obstacle, but it is also the way forward.

WHAT I LEARNED FROM SIP: SHELTERING IN PLACE

Zaneta Varnado Johns

Half full, half empty: either way, you're the other half of my cup.
God's timing is incredibly punctual.
I crave social interaction, but I covet stillness.
Quietness is loud and very much appreciated.
Ample space is a generous gift.
I won't be well until you're well.
A child's infinite wonder makes the worst things bearable.
Everyone has a pearl of wisdom to offer.
If you haven't found joy, try looking inside.
Simple things are being discovered; thank you, SIP!
Be intentional; connection comes in various forms.
I like beautiful things, but I don't need all of them.
If you're troubled by painful thoughts, remove the thorn.
Life's storms bring rain. When the sun returns, seek out the rainbows.
Wake up expecting to make a difference.
Imagine the impending smile of someone you plan to help.
Don't ignore your talents; when you're ready for them, they might be
    gone.
Passion is everything they said it is.
Kind words are soothing; hug someone with your words.
Let's make "love" our next pandemic!

THE REALITY OF DENIAL

Sallie Moffitt

My phone rang. It was my younger sister. She couldn't take our 83-year-old mother to receive her COVID shot and asked me to do it. My shoulders dropped. I sighed and reluctantly agreed.

You see, my mother and I had never been close. Our fractured relationship began when I was a child, and my abusive alcoholic father dominated our home. My mother buried her head in the Bible and ignored what my father was doing, leaving me and my sister to fend for ourselves.

In addition, I wasn't sure the shot was necessary. Many government leaders claimed the virus was a hoax and more people died each year from influenza than the coronavirus. Were they right?

My sister signed our elderly parent up for the vaccine in mid-December, but an appointment wasn't available until January. The Dallas County Health Department scheduled my mother to receive her first shot the afternoon of January 20th, the day Joseph R. Biden, Jr. was to be sworn in as our 46th President.

On the day of my mother's appointment, I drove her to the Fair Park vaccination site in Dallas. Numerous signs along the road stated that the COVID-19 vaccination was only available to those 75 years and older.

We entered the main gate of the Fair Park entertainment complex and stopped at the guardhouse. I lowered my window. A volunteer firefighter checked the birthdate on my mother's driver's license to verify her age. He handed her some paperwork and motioned for us to drive forward, where helpful volunteers guided us through the sprawling grounds. When we arrived at a half-empty parking lot, we parked alongside the other cars, trucks, and SUVs.

As instructed, my elderly mother and I stood beside our car and waited for a golf cart to shuttle us to the Grand Place exhibition hall for her shot. Up and down the rows of parked automobiles, elderly Americans in masks and winter coats waited beside their vehicles with their family members and caregivers. Some able-bodied folks, like my mother, stood on their own two feet, while others sat in wheelchairs, or leaned on walkers or canes. They waited under overcast skies with pages of paperwork clutched in their hands. They waited in the cold drizzle for friendly volunteers to transport them to the Grand Place building about a half-mile away. They waited on this gray day to receive their shot of the controversial vaccine.

When the golf carts arrived, many struggled to get in them. Caregivers and family members gripped their aging arms, holding them steady, as the older generation climbed into their seats. A six-person electric cart stopped near us. I helped my mother board the small vehicle and sat beside her on the bench seat in the rear.

Not far from us, a man opened the passenger door to his sedan to reveal a middle-aged woman slumped in the front seat, her seatbelt holding her limp body in place. The paralyzed woman wore blue jeans with a stiff crease, a fashionable red button-down shirt and a matching ruby-red coat, her auburn hair perfectly brushed and styled. The man with the woman, a burly guy with graying brown hair, confirmed with our driver that wheelchairs were not allowed on the cart. Our driver reassured him that one would be available at the entrance to Grand Place.

I watched the man scoop the woman from her seat, cradling her in his arms like a baby, and carry her to the cart. He set her on the bench seat in front of us and positioned her body so she couldn't fall over. He then sat in the seat beside her, wrapping his arm around her shoulders, securing her body in place. The man smiled at the quadriplegic woman and said, "Honey, we're on our way to get your shot. Won't be long now." The woman stared blankly ahead.

Tears welled in my eyes and rolled down my cheeks. I brushed them away. The bleak reality I saw today reminded me of being a child in my abusive home. I remembered being overwhelmed with fear and hiding under the honeysuckle vines in the back corner of our yard. Lying on the ground, I had heaved sobs of sorrow from the pit of my soul, frightened by the brutality of my father.

At last the golf cart transported us to the front doors of Grand Place, a 55,000-square-foot exhibition hall with tables full of nurses administering shots. All around me, elderly people shuffled towards the building. Health care workers pushed patients in beds, IV drip bags hanging from the side, through the automatic doors. Most of the people I saw weren't well enough to leave the nursing home or other facility where they resided. Yet here they were, under the gloomy skies, waiting for their shot at being vaccinated, waiting for their shot at beating the pandemic.

On January 20, 2021, over 401,000 people had died from COVID-19. America was averaging 4,000 deaths a day from the deadly virus—with no end in sight. Each day over a hundred thousand people became infected and thousands more died. The future appeared grim.

The despair on the sad, sagging faces around me told me the coronavirus was real. These people didn't care about the side effects, the politics, the excuses. They had watched family members, friends and neighbors contract the disease and die painful deaths alone in the hospital, hooked up to a ventilator. They didn't want to suffer the same fate and were willing to do whatever was necessary to protect themselves from the virus.

I thought about the American leaders who pretended everything was fine. They distorted medical facts, downplayed the consequences, and blamed other causes for the casualties. The desperation I saw today contradicted everything they said.

I wanted to tell those leaders that denying the pandemic wouldn't make it go away. Growing up, my mother ignored my father's behavior and justified his actions. Her living in denial didn't make the abuse go away, but it did make it worse. Her refusal to accept the truth allowed the harmful situation to continue and escalate until it destroyed my childhood.

Once I became an adult, I could no longer escape the trauma of my past. I had to face the lies and half-truths pounded into my head and open my eyes to reality. When the truth bubbled to the surface, I had to learn not to suppress it, but to acknowledge it and deal with it. I had to face the facts and examine my fears. When I did, I began to heal.

My elderly mother received her vaccination with no side effects. Despite our differences, I was glad she had her shot. She was now protected from the virus. She had a fighting chance at surviving the pandemic. We exited the building, and another golf cart carried us back to our car.

A month later, I took my mother to receive her second shot. With the newly elected Biden administration now governing our country, appointments for shots were easier to get. Vaccination sites were popping up everywhere. The Fair Park vaccination site had been converted to a drive-thru, like many others in our area. With this shot, my mother didn't even get out of the car. She simply lowered her window, and a nurse administered the shot to her arm.

This improvement stirred a tinge of hope in my soul. Maybe America was accepting the truth about the coronavirus. Maybe America was facing the reality of the pandemic. Maybe America was beginning to heal.

A few days after my mother got her second shot, I received a notice that I qualified for the vaccine. I made an appointment for my husband and me, and we received our shots. We felt honored to be doing our part in combating COVID-19.

Taking my mother for her vaccination changed my perception of the virus. It helped me see how people have used the pandemic to perpetuate their own fears. What were the people who refused to get vaccinated afraid of? What truth were they avoiding? Were they using it as an excuse to ignore our changing world? Were they dismissing COVID to keep from facing their own insecurities? Or was it simply easier to deny the reality of a pandemic?

TEACHER OF THE YEAR

Cynthia F. Davidson

What sort of students are we?
That is the question.
When the Teacher stalks our Earth
silent, invisible, and most of all
capricious.

With the ruler held behind Her back
She mimics our range of capabilities
to be dullards, showoffs, stalwarts,
geniuses, or ignoramuses.

"Pride goeth before a fall," She teaches
tripping up the good as well as
the mighty braggarts.
Epic takedowns, like double loads
of jumbo jets falling from the skies,
as if 50 Americans dying every hour
weren't enough to command

our attention. Yet still some deny they're
in class, shut their ears to Teacher and lessons.

We must be teachable, or else.
The maw of Eternity awaits.
Whether we cower or glower
the End shall be the same.
It's only a matter of when...
and where...and how long.

Live to learn another day.
Give the Teacher Her due.
But never invite Her to dinner,
nor to the bar or café. She goes
where she will, smacking heads,
stealing sense of taste and smell
before taking your breath away.

You ignore Her at your peril
never sure if you're asymptomatic
a carrier, or a mild case, or a maker
of the deadly grade. Listen up class.
Change your tune and alter your ways.
Wise up or shut up.
This could be your final exam.

MAKING LEMONADE

Ariela Zucker

I reflect on the months of sheltering at home. Trying to follow the ever-changing guidelines. Watching smug TV anchors interviewing health officials who appear knowledgeable despite their total ignorance. I cringe inside. But then I remind myself of the biggest hurdle I overcame in the past year and give myself a pat on the back. Reaching out without a physical touch, I managed to stay connected to the people I care about.

My big personal victory was letting Zoom enter my life. To me, this was a lesson of overcoming a deep-rooted fear of anything computer related. Feeling awkward and clumsy facing a screen and looking at my face for a whole hour or more. Dealing with the mysterious language of codes and symbols and varied apparatus needed to enter a Zoom class.

To top it all, I carried a deep trauma connected to distance learning. Though during pre-pandemic times, the pain felt fresh, as if it just happened. The Zoom challenge made this memory surface, and as I reviewed it, I realized that I never came to terms with it.

It happened during my first encounter with video conferencing—in a creative writing class given by my local college. That morning I walked into room 156 and was faced with two big screens and an empty room.

"Hello," I said firmly to no one in particular, since there was no one there, and my face extremely enlarged on the right screen was the only response. I sat and waited for something to happen.

At 9:00 a.m. sharp, the second screen came to life, and a lively picture of a teacher in front of a class appeared.

"Wait!" It was a 'real' teacher speaking to a few students. Almost immediately, a short elderly woman walked into the room and handed me a giant remote.

"Sorry, but I have to leave to feed my horses," she said. "I'll be back soon. In the meantime, hold this remote and un-press the mute button when you want to be heard."

"You'll be fine," she added, looking at the total confusion on my face.

Trusted with the remote, I turned back to the face of the teacher. The screen, to my surprise, split into five smaller squares, each presenting a different group of people.

"Let's see if everyone is here," the teacher said as she proceeded to go through a list of towns.

Each of them, I understood, was represented by one of the small squares. People smiled and nodded, and so did I, being the only representative of my city.

"Good," the teacher commented with a cheery voice as if this in and of itself was a significant achievement. Then she went on to deliver a lengthy description of the syllabus, its structure, future assignments, final tests, and so on. I tried to follow, only halfway through, I got an eerie feeling, something did not seem right, and as a confirmation of my sensation, one of the small squares on the big screen turned black.

I looked around; the teacher kept talking. The students in the other squares listened intently, yet that nudging feeling.

"Hey!" I raised my hand and waved.

"Can you see me? Hear me?" nothing, no reaction.

"Hey, I am here. Do you see me?"

I tried again, this time in a louder voice, adding hopping up and down, still nothing.

On the screen, the class went on. No one seemed to notice my absence.

In desperation, I turned to the remote, zoomed in, zoomed out, raised the volume, lowered it, and pressed a few other random buttons for good luck, still nothing.

"How are you doing? '' The elderly lady suddenly showed up by my side, "All is fine?"

"No one can see or hear me," I admitted to my failure.

"I am sure all is fine," she said.

"No, it is not," I pleaded, "see for yourself."

And she did. After a few minutes of hand waving and some jumping, she resorted to screaming, "Hey, you there!" I watched, enchanted; I knew it would not work.

"OK," she said, finally. "Something must be wrong; I will be back," and off she went.

Two minutes later, both screens went black.

I held my breath, careful not to interfere and worsen the situation. I clearly was the one at fault since there was no one else present.

Five minutes went by, and suddenly, just like they died, the two screens flickered back to life, and behind them, triumphant, the short elderly lady, my rescuer.

"See, I told you it is going to be fine," she beamed at my sullen face, and without another word, handed me the dreaded remote.

Feeling somewhat reassured by her trust, I pressed the mute button and only then gathered enough courage to look at the two screens.

I couldn't believe it. On the big screen, the class went on as if nothing had happened. Looking at the teacher, a sickening feeling came over me. The teacher did not miss me. The words went on and on in my head, gathering hot energy with each repeating round.

"She did not miss me, overlooked my nonexistence, ignored my black screen. My misery, being all alone in an empty room, holding a huge remote, did not send any waves of distress."

I looked at my enraged face on the smaller screen, stood up, picked up my notebook and pen, and a minute before walking out of the room, pressed the remote on mute one last time

This was a lemon. I never attempted distance learning again. But with Zoom, I transformed this anger into fresh-squeezed lemonade.

I learned how to Zoom. I mastered the mysterious language needed to enter a Zoom class. It felt like magic. From time to time, things can still go wrong. I am left outside in the cold unyielding cyberspace, banging on the doors pleading for help in an indifferent world. But I know that that's the price of taking risks, and the reward is communication, and that invigorates me like a bittersweet cold lemonade.

ABECEDARIAN WISDOM

Zaneta Varnado Johns

Affirm your beliefs and pray for a
Better world of good intentions
Consciously care about mother earth … let us
Do good deeds … make room for
Every person without fear of scarcity
Free our hearts of hatred, our minds of
Greed … accept that all people
Have merit … our words and actions are
Instrumental to humanity's resurgence …
Joyfully extend your true self—be
Kind … be generous
Love intently, knowing what really
Matters … suspend judgment
No one exists above the other … how
Often will you reach out—or reach back
Prepare for and expect success …
Query your thoughts for ways to show
Respect … always, demand respect
Settle for nothing less

Trust cautiously and responsibly ... seek
Understanding when tensions rise
Very soon you will appreciate
Why these things are crucial ... a
Xeric-like mind
Yearns for empathy, the only path to our
Zealous collective quest for love!

LIFE AFTER COVID?

Marion Hunt

COVID has been a fearless and powerful enemy of the people of the world. In many places, we diligently continue to strive to develop the weapons needed to defeat the enemy, but all through the pandemic, more people have died than most of us could ever have imagined. And while the emotional pain of loss pressed upon our hearts, forced us into isolation, and challenged our zest for life, it also brought families together, and reminded us how to play Monopoly and hopscotch. It encouraged us to look at our bookshelves holding tomes long waiting to be read, now being opened and enjoyed.

Many good cooks emerged from COVID. While complaining about weight gain, new recipes out of old ingredients were discovered and enjoyed, and desserts were revised and created to be healthier and sometimes sweeter.

Our lives craved sweetness.

Technology brought us closer to friends and family all over the world. Zoom meetings include loving shared times, educational workshops, historical overviews, art, music, and other creative inventions.

Employees who were lucky enough to have jobs, didn't have to dress to go to work, and could often work on their chosen time schedules. Busy parents had to juggle the challenges of multi-tasking responsibilities of family and employment. Younger single people and childless households found that being home opened them up and allowed for new ideas and improvements in their jobs.

Education suffered – more for some, less for others. While it would have been much better for students to have live interactions with their friends and teachers, at least they were safe. With the increase in vaccines and vaccinations, schools can schedule reopening.

Having been a classroom teacher for twenty-five years, I was pleased that many parents got a real introduction to what it takes to be a teacher. Of course, to truly experience the teacher's life, they would have to multiply their one child by twenty or more, and those other nineteen who were not theirs would have varying abilities and disabilities, while reacting to this weird life with a jumble of emotions, physical actions, heightened visibility, and closeted minds. Some adults will have enjoyed the freedom of being home and having more time with their children. Others will have had the added burden of finding and learning to use a computer while they hunted for enough food to feed their hungry families.

A frightened person might have frozen in the midst of all this. The individual would have looked for a bright spot outside while staring down at the ever-growing dark shadow that was deepening the reality of the enormous number of deaths, and the uncertainty of life going forward.

Well, I am not a pessimist, but I am a realist. Not all people will have gotten smarter because of this pandemic. Some will not have learned from our mistakes. Environmentally created and man-made disasters will continue to lengthen and intensify. Tornadoes, hurricanes, floods, freezing weather, and lengthening, out-of-control, tragic wildfires will get worse until scientists and the citizens of the world agree to participate in working toward positive changes. Our government is wobbly and confused. Those who should be working as a team are challenging each other. The fighting and competition is fierce and anger-filled.

Like the old Weeble toy with its rounded body and small flat spot on the bottom to insure stability, hopefully it will wobble but it won't fall down. Hate still darkens our world, but people are more outspoken and demanding their human rights. Police body cameras and citizen cell phones will help to tell stories of that part of human nature we would prefer not to see or know. But we do see and know, and it hurts.

Because of these events, the shouting will keep getting louder. The lines of angry marchers will get longer.

We cannot blame COVID for this unfortunate aspect of life. We must grasp onto what is best in the world. We must confront the naysayers. We must never, in any way, forget our mission to destroy the evil in our world caused by humans and nature, so that generations after us will benefit from our movement toward a better future.

What will life be post-COVID? The story will join the history books whose authors will decide its interpretation.

With all its sadness, ugliness, crime and hostility, Life also proved that we have many heroes among us. We have discovered people who will give up their jackets to strangers suffering in a cold winter wind, and those who will join the living in this world with their pencils and erasers to keep improving the picture.

March and make noise. Be safe, and live our best lives.

MISSION RESET

Dr. Lisa Baron

I am scared, entering Phase 1 of world re-entry, post-vaccine. For the past fifteen months, I have sat at my own control panel, attempting to navigate through the maze of Pandemic 2020. During this journey, I have run into a series of twists, turns, and potholes.

Today I stand in line to board a plane, carrying the usual suspects: dog-eared novel, 3 oz. toothpaste, and a sweater for my Chicago journey. I feel more secure seeing a tall, masked pilot entering the cockpit. I have turned my fate over to him and his crew, as well as to science and a vaccine that I hope guards me from serious illness, and worse. I am cautiously enlarging my circle to strangers in a stranger land.

I watch the other passengers as we board the plane. They come in all shapes and sizes. Some have double masks, some have a "bearded mask" under their chin, a few have no masks at all. I see passengers decorated in tattoos and piercings, some with suitcases displaying their beliefs on stickers and slogans. Some of the stickers and slogans make me feel afraid, judgmental, and annoyed. I saw one slogan that said, "Science is often wrong," and another that stated, "I decide about the mask. Period."

I am disappointed in myself that I am focusing on our differences, yet not considering our commonalities. Perhaps some of these passengers also haven't seen their families and friends from afar. Maybe they have longed to hug their loved ones, after tearfully seeing them through screen video calls for too many months, just like me. Who have they missed? Who have they lost? Who are these strangers in this strange land? I want to dial down on judgment and dial up on curiosity. There is so much that I don't know.

I board the plane, squeezing through the narrow aisle while wheeling my new purple suitcase to my row. I bought this new suitcase to commemorate my maiden flight, after so many months of lockdown. I'm particularly mindful of not bumping into a seated passenger. I arrive at my row and am thankful the suitcase fits under my seat. There's some comfort in having it close, a small sense of security during this surreal time.

I feel embarrassed that I am squeamish about sitting next to strangers. I decide to pivot in my mind to curiosity. I say hello to the people on both sides of me with my eyes, as our masks muffle our full expressions. Having made the connections, I buckle myself in.

The pilot makes the familiar announcement. "Please keep your seatbelts fastened in the event of unexpected turbulence. We will be flying at _____ feet". (I never listen to that part, not loving to fly to begin with.) And then he says. "Please keep your mask on throughout the flight – this is required. And one more thing. Please show extra kindness and acceptance on this flight. We all need it, today, and always."

I gaze out the window at the billowing clouds as I replay the pilot's wisdom. "Extra kindness and acceptance," he said. Sounds easy enough to cast a smile (with my eyes) and converse with a masked stranger sitting next to me, who I'll likely never encounter again.

Sometimes it's easier to be more accepting of people I don't know. I can't do a playback of relationship blips, or stings or hurts. I don't ache from memories.

The pandemic has brought me to an introspective pause, gazing into the mirror of my own feelings, thoughts, and narratives. I think about those narratives and how I might rewrite the ones that no longer serve me. Perhaps they never did.

Two hours later, and in excited anticipation of reuniting with my family, I feel the plane gliding into its descent. I begin to see the tops of city buildings through the fog cover. As we get closer, the fog lifts so that I recognize some of the building's names. Though I've taken this flight many times, somehow this landing is different. It's as if my fog is lifting, as well.

As the months unfold after the initial pandemic, I find myself in a world that continues to have COVID's variants, judgment, and uncertainty. Our world needs a reset. Starting with my own.

REIMAGINING THE WORLD

Cynthia F. Davidson

After so much catastrophe, the world must be reimagined, by us all. To keep things simple, we will use only a few pebbles to describe this process. And you will need to collect them.

Return to Nature to do this. Take a very deliberate walk. Look for smooth stones that speak to you in some way. Take only the rocks that want to go with you. If you pay prayerful attention, and seek their counsel, their silent replies will be discernable.

For each stone you take, leave something in return. This is a universal law – give and take. Whether a strand of hair, a song, a pinch of tobacco or cornmeal…when receiving, even a rock, we give in turn. This keeps the Universe in Balance. Gather rocks in a range of colors, and rough proportion, sizewise.

Remember what these pebbles are going to represent, the rules that govern everything and everyone in the Universe. Once you learn them you can teach them.

When you have at least five handpicked pebbles, rinse them in pond, stream, or sea. Then find a clear place to sit. Put the stones down beside you to dry. Remain seated, on the Earth, until you feel well grounded.

Imagine the ground rules for a better world. You will use five stones to pose its base. Reconstruct your foundation. Which bedrock principles would you like to guide your life? Lay down those basics. Choose the laws you want to live by.

Face North while you sit on the ground to work with your stones. If you do not have a compass, you can make one with your rocks. Which Direction did the Sun rise in this morning? That will be to your right when you face North. The Sun sets in the West, which will be to your left.

Now choose the best-proportioned, smoothest stone. Put it down in front of you to form the center of a circle, a sacred space. This is the lynchpin. You will use it to realign everything in the Universe. It stands for Balance. Reflect on a world without Balance. What happens when we deny this rule? Consider everything the principle of Balance means, in the broadest sense. Our Sun star centers our solar system. Our planet Earth orbits it in Balance. Balancing work is dynamic. It requires we be alert to what helps or harms it. Equanimity. Fairness. Justice.

Pick another pebble to represent Right Action. Lay it on the East side, where the Sun rises. If this stone happens to be yellow, the color of the rising Sun, all the better. This is the light of Enlightenment. Let this rock represent thought and intellect, the wisdom of deep respect for Nature's grand design. Right Action comes when we study Nature's Laws.

Lay your third stone in the South, nearest to you. This is the sign of Trust, when the heart's truths are regularly consulted. When heart and head are in agreement, human beings are not conflicted.

Your fourth stone goes on your left side. It represents the West, dusk and your Higher Purpose. When your light goes out, and you go to the Other Side, this will be what others mention when talking about what you stood for, and what you accomplished with your time on this planet.

Lastly, lay down your True North stone. Set it like a star in your crown. This is for Integrity. This overarching guidance integrates all your parts, so your life will align in harmony, with others as well as your conscience. Stay conscious. Together we can reimagine our world.

AUGUST IS WANING

Shawn Essed

Damp. Dew covered grass. Orange sun rising behind the trees across the street. Cicadas buzz. Air conditioning units cut on and off. Occasional traffic in the distance. The cat rolls on the concrete and meows, asking me to pet her. I do. Then I lean back in the front porch rocker with my coffee and toast. It's time to decide.

Adulthood has clouded my mind, layered it with fear, guilt, indecision and restlessness. "Listen to the nudge," they say. "Which one?" I wonder. "The one in alignment with your values. Be your authentic self," they answer. Who the hell is that?

Two years ago I knew that I had to change something in my life. My back constantly hurt, my marriage made me sad, my oldest kids seemed depressed and stuck, and my youngest seemed lonely. I went to a therapist. She asked, "What do you want?" I had a comfortable home in a decent neighborhood, a kind husband, kids who talked to me, two low paying, but fun jobs. One of my sisters called my life perfect on several occasions. I practiced gratitude and it made me feel like a royal jerk to be restless when I had a list of blessings a mile long. I meditated, talked to friends, family, and co-workers. Something had to give, but what? Indecision paralyzed me precisely because I had so much to be grateful for. I had too much to lose.

Change came for me in the form of a pandemic. It came for all of us. About eighteen months ago, governors across America mandated a massive shutdown of businesses and schools to slow the spread of the coronavirus. Don't socialize. Limit shopping (how un-American!) Work from home if you can. My work as a yoga teacher and banquet server was considered nonessential, so except for my college classes, which moved online, I was largely unemployed.

People around the world suffered loss of income, loneliness, overwhelm, and sometimes deadly sickness due to the pandemic. But for me, it was a staycation. I did yoga and jigsaw puzzles. I hiked, baked, gardened, and took an online course with my sister. I talked on the phone. Since the bars were closed, my husband came directly home from work every day. Who knew he got off so early! The big kids weren't socializing, so after work they were home for meals and watching movies. Other people suffered. Older people especially were lonely and afraid. Hospitals were overcrowded. Parents juggled childcare with working at home. I relaxed, healed, and felt happier than I had been for many years. The pandemic was restoring my family, my home, and my back.

I look up from my journal; sip my coffee from my tall blue mug. The neighborhood begins to stir. A car passes. A child whines. A man walks his dog and we wave to each other, "Morning."

As Covid cases decreased, businesses reopened and kids went back to school. The first day that bars reopened, my husband stopped for a drink on his way home from work. When he started staying out on the weekends again, something in me collapsed. "I was so happy when the bars were closed. Now we're going back to the old life and it makes me want to cry," I confessed. He never replied, but now he usually comes home before dark.

With social distancing and mask mandates, I returned weekdays to part-time teaching yoga. My students were happy to be in class and I felt I was doing some good in the world. Now my class load is about half of what it was before. Yoga is only healthy in moderation. Though banquet serving was fun, my back said no, and I wanted to savor the weekends with the family, so I didn't return to that job. I'm prioritizing family and health...except financial health. My bank account is bleeding. Resting, hiking, and playing Mario Kart with the kid do not pay for a comfortable home, even a small one.

I stop thinking to pet the gray tabby. She's small and soft. The big black and white cat joins us. They touch nose to nose, then part ways. Am I overthinking again? Am I fighting with life when I should be savoring it? Is this nudge for necessary change or just discontentment? Can we tighten our belts and live on this income?

A few years ago, I went back to college as a student. I planned to apply to a Physical Therapy Assistant program, and I needed a few prerequisites. I started with Biology 101, but after two weeks, I chose to attend a weekend yoga workshop instead of studying for my first test. On the day of the test I headed to the registrar's office and dropped the class. As I walked back to my car that day I cried. There was no way to pass the test without studying. And without an A, there was no getting into the competitive PTA program.

Occasionally over the years I've applied for jobs – admin, librarian, receptionist, payroll. Apparently a thirty-year-old BA degree is worth very little. I received emails thanking me for my interest, and informing me that someone with more suitable skills and experience was selected. Then, a few weeks ago, I got an interview for a job as part-time physical therapy aide, a very entry-level position. When they asked me my availability, I gave them hours when I'm usually resting or taking care of my youngest child or my home, my so-called free time. How does one balance rest with financial stability?

They've offered me the job, and it's time for me to accept or decline it. Accepting it would mean two days per week that I wouldn't be here to see my youngest after school, and I'd have to trust his father to stay sober after work to take him to karate class. He insists that he will. His track record says he won't. My daughter offered to help at least once a week. Bless her. That could make all the difference. Once a week the youngest would have to get himself off to school in the morning. At 13, I wonder if he's old enough to do that. If I like this job, perhaps I'd go back to school and apply for that program after all. My friends encourage me. "You would be so good at that!" I lament, "But I'd be in my mid-50's when I finished! Will anyone hire me?" If I decline the job, I'd have to keep searching for another or increase the yoga load again. And if I keep pushing my back to do more twisting, bending, and stretching, it will not heal. Still the pay is so low, it barely feels worth giving up time with my son, with my journal, with nature.

No matter what I choose, change will happen. Sickness, death, job loss. Health, fun, opportunity. They're all in the cards.

The August sun has risen and it's getting hot out here on the porch. A hummingbird sips from the morning glories and the petunias. It hovers close to me, then zips off. God, I love August. I always hate to see it go. Yet I rejoice in September. And there is my answer. I love so much in my life that I'm terrified to loosen my grip on any of it. Covid has reminded me of my values – family and stability, but also learning and growth. It's just a part-time job, but it feels significant because I am so uncertain, so scared. I have loved each season of my life and now I am reminded that this next season will also hold beauty. Gratitude is my nature. That's my authentic self.

I go inside the house and up to my room where I turn on my laptop and open my email. "Yes, I am happy to accept your job offer." It doesn't matter if it leads me back to school or if it's a dead end. All that matters is that I'm peeling off a layer of fear, indecision, and insecurity.

MY PANDEMIC BUBBLE

Janice Airhart

What you don't know, until you've scored the last 18-roll Mega-pack of Charmin on the shelf at your local H-E-B, is how divine a pandemic shutdown will be. For the mathematically challenged, a Mega-pack is the equivalent of 72 *regular* rolls, which haven't been available for purchase since 1983. But no matter. For introverts like me, the toilet paper quest notwithstanding, early and heroic efforts to waylay Covid-19 via barricading myself behind a tower of Clorox Wipes canisters and a double-bolted front door proved oddly invigorating.

I don't mean to minimize a ghastly disease. Even when the virus isn't lethal, lingering effects are pernicious. Coronavirus doesn't respect where you fall on the extraversion scale. At the same time, I reveled in all that sudden *quiet*. I realize I'm fortunate in that I have a front door to double lock, no job to truck to, and I was sequestered with a couple of companions: my husband and our canine fur factory. I did miss indoor visits with our son, daughter-in-law and granddaughter, a half-hour's drive away, but we managed backyard visits when the weather cooperated. I can't recommend conducting the annual gift exchange amidst the wafting automotive smells of the garage on Christmas morning, masked and six feet apart, but the red tablecloth and miniature Christmas tree on the air hockey table was a nice touch. We're a creative family; we found ways to be together.

I'm fortunate in other ways, too. My extravert friends suffered from in-person interaction withdrawal that didn't afflict me. Instead, we connected digitally. One close friend refused to communicate outside two-hour telephone conversations—an introvert's kryptonite. The rest, all residing in other states, settled for shorter virtual gatherings. For a somewhat obsessive, solitary-minded brooder like me, in between enjoying brief congenial exchanges, I was free to create my own diversions, on my own timetable. As 2020 dragged on, additional areas of advantage presented themselves as well.

1. Recently retired, I was up to my collarbones in community volunteering when Covid hit: reading to first graders at our neighborhood school, manning the reception desk at the county children's advocacy center, GED tutoring, and ESL teaching. All that time in the company of others was exhausting. Once the programs were scrapped, I devoted myself to making up for some of the naps I'd refused as a child.
2. 70,000 words. It took six months to suss out threads of essays I'd written a dozen years before and to connect themes and scenes into a book-length memoir. Never mind that the first draft resembled an amorphous, vomitous mass. Now, after a year of revision, it reads more or less as I intended; I just need a publisher to concede its brilliance.
3. Old hobbies. I dusted off crochet hooks and sewing machine to fashion usable goods. While the beanies, coasters, and tote bags had limited appreciative recipients, creating them was refreshing after years peddling unwanted products to teenagers: "How to correct fused sentences and structure thesis statements," for instance, or "How to save their parents

money on their college tuition by enrolling in the free high school and college dual credit offerings."

4. "If it grows, it goes." This maxim characterized what could be composted from the mounds of organic material our small household discarded. I invested in a dual-chambered tumbling composter and researched how to "cook" nutrient-rich detritus to spread over my garden. Nothing like plunging elbow-deep in *rotting* vegetable matter in the service of *new* vegetable matter.

5. Less traffic. Less gas guzzled. Less time on the road. Enough said.

6. At first, I resisted the video component of digital conversations. I soon learned to value the pluses of making myself presentable from the shoulders up, sans makeup, in shorts and flip-flops. Headshots also disguised my swelling waistline, thanks to another Covid pastime: breadmaking. Everyone knows the camera adds ten pounds, but I don't need the visual reminder.

Despite unexpected bonuses of the Covid pandemic, and post-vaccine, I'm eager for the freedom of ordinary comings and goings. I sincerely want this virus vanquished. Nevertheless, I'm grateful for the reflection time and accomplishments the pandemic bubble afforded. This introvert will miss social distancing from strangers. I'll miss mumbling softly into my mask as I recite my grocery list and wander the aisles (one way) at H-E-B without self-consciousness. I'll stock up on Charmin while I can and prepare myself for the end of this semi-solitary interlude with resignation and guilty regret.

PERSONAL EXPLORATION

Jo Virgil

Life is a journey, not a destination.
Every step is a metaphor, but one with no map.
Sometimes we hike through the wilderness,
Sometimes we join friends on the playground,
Sometimes we fly up into the clouds to find rain,
Or fly beyond them to find sunshine.

When the COVID virus came looking for me,
I shuttered myself alone at home, for me and for others.
I learned how to have groceries delivered to my door,
How to meet up with friends via Zoom,
How to tap deeper into books, into podcasts and videos.
A new kind of life was settling in.

And then loneliness started to settle in.

The Pollyanna inside me seemed to be dying.
My journey through life felt like it had come to an halt,
Like I had been locked in a cage with no key.
I, could see my friends' faces online and share stories,
But that seemed like a pretend dream, not real.
How can I wake up? I kept asking myself.

And then the next journey began, a new field of exploration.
My loneliness kept tapping me from inside,
Asking me to come explore a deeper reality,
To discover myself, my meaning, my mind, and my soul,
Wound together in ways I'd not sensed before.
Inside, I found the true meaning of peace and joy.

COVID pointed me into a journey I'd never traveled so deeply.

BEACONS OF HOPE

Sara Etgen-Baker

I often witnessed my mother, vexed and overcome by unresolved problems and unmet needs, throw up her hands in an *I give up* gesture. "I'm at my wits' end," she'd exclaim, her face becoming pinched with tension-filled expression. Imagine my shock when I looked in the mirror one day and saw that same pinched, tension-filled expression on *my* face. I was apparently at my "wits' end," ready to give up. *How had I gotten here?*

I remember being hopeful on New Year's Day 2020, standing on the deck of a new year, unaware I'd soon be on a storm-tossed sea. Then COVID arrived, its powerful winds tossing my ship back and forth. I was unable to find my sea legs, staggering across the deck like a drunken sailor. Increased violence, social unrest, and divisiveness arrived, quickly tattering my ship's sails, ripping apart and fraying the American culture that had been my anchor. Personal freedoms and normal activities stopped, replaced with mask mandates, lockdowns, isolation, and social distancing. Wave after wave crashed upon the deck. The world seemed distant, surreal, and chaotic. I was lost at sea, alone, frightened, and overwhelmed, struggling just to hold on, let alone navigate the turbulent ocean.

A contentious election brought further turmoil, rendering me helpless and vulnerable. Storm after storm arrived, exposing overreaching, incompetent government officials, media propaganda, misinformation, censorship, and government corruption. A new White House administration brought rapid change and increased uncertainty and doubt.

I was desperate, clinging to the mast, hoping that the COVID vaccine would reduce the fear, ease the lockdowns, end the isolation, and return precious personal freedoms. Such was not the case. Instead, I arrived on the shore of a new, unfamiliar reality: a less prosperous, less open, and less free world—a world that was out of my control or influence. *Normalcy,* as I understood it, had been completely upended; I feared it would never return. There was no escaping this reality, no help, and apparently no deliverance.

I was at my "wits' end"—a hopeless victim filled with helplessness, anxiety, unresolved anger, and mild depression. I was experiencing what some called the *echo pandemic,* and there was no vaccine nor a quick cure for it. What was I to do? Fortunately, I remembered a story my father told me when I was an angry teenager lashing out at others, consumed by some adolescent injustice over which I had no control.

"A long time ago a wise old Cherokee warrior sat around a campfire with his grandchildren. 'A battle rages inside me,' he told them. 'It's a terrible fight between two wolves. One wolf represents deceit, anger, fear, hate, and hopelessness. The other stands for truth, joy, peace, love, and hope.'

The old man looked at the children with a firm stare. 'This same fight goes on inside you and every other person.'

The grandchildren sat in silence and thought about the story for quite some time. Finally, one child asked his grandfather, 'Which wolf wins?'

The old Cherokee replied, 'The one you feed.'"

I'd been feeding the wrong wolf! What a powerful realization! No wonder I was angry, anxious, and helpless. Flickering through this realization, like froth on the ocean waves, was that intuitive response hardwired into us humans: resilience—the innate capacity of self-leadership and ability to navigate challenges. I'd sacrificed my resilience along with the power of the energy that comes with self-leadership. I had to reclaim my resiliency. *But how?*

I had to make a decision: either assert myself and leave the tumultuous sea—dock my ship and come ashore where my resiliency lay waiting for me—or remain lost at sea, passively clinging to what *was* and permitting uncertainty, fear, and rage to drown me. I came ashore, slowly accepting that uncertainty is a given. I grieved the *old normal* then let it go. Instead of concentrating on things over which I had no control, I focused on things I could control, like my eating and thinking habits. I stopped using food to cope and to comfort myself and chose better eating habits—eliminating high-calorie foods and unnecessary snacking, and reducing portion sizes. I walked outside in the sunshine every day observing nature and taking delight in it.

I invested in myself, *unfollowing* and disconnecting from toxic people and from those with whom I didn't share similar cultural or political views. I disassociated from situations or circumstances that weren't good for my emotional and mental stability. I also limited the amount of news I read and evaluated the television shows I watched, eliminating those prone to violence, aggression, deception, antisocial behavior, and negativity. I rediscovered living in the present, listening to piano music, and reading for pleasure.

I reframed my interpretations of adversities, asking myself, "What good can come from this adversity?" Seeking goodness took me away from my negative, claustrophobic thinking about current crises and reminded me of the big picture: the blessings and comforts of current moments.

I gradually became more resilient and emotionally stronger than I ever imagined. That strength gave rise to a fervent return to my long-forgotten passion: writing and storytelling. Stories had always been my language; as a child, creating them was my way of expressing the wonder and possibility around me. As a teenager, writing in my diary was my way of processing the world. As a young adult, I believed life was more than what it was on the surface. There was some bigger truth to be explored, something yearning to be understood, something beyond me begging for expression, something that *mattered*: a story waiting to be told.

Most people didn't see stories the way I did. I'd close a book or come out of a movie, and the world would be shining because of a truth I understood or the creative power I'd just experienced. Others shrugged, "Yeah, it was fun." For them, stories were about entertainment and escapism. Despite the disillusionment I sometimes felt, I wrote, convinced stories *must be* more than a soporific drug, numbing our minds against the difficulties, confusion, and injustices of our lives.

I returned to writing, hoping to make some sense of the world I was experiencing. I wrote without thinking further than the next line. Initially, my words were nothing more than a penned medication, dispersing my pain and healing my broken spirit. But the more I wrote, the more convinced I became that there was some truth that needed to be explored, something more that yearned to be understood, something beyond me begging for expression. *But what was it?*

I occasionally pondered: *In the grand scheme of things is writing really **all** that important? What truths, if any, do stories reveal, or are they merely "roses and rainbows" offering little more than mind-numbing escapism? Are they beneficial? If so, how? Do they change the world for the better? What hope do stories offer for a future beyond COVID and 2020?*

I determined that all stories are fundamentally *truths*—even when the author didn't intend them to be so, even when she's unaware of it, even when the readers or viewers are unaware. A story is a statement. If it is to ring true, what it says must reflect a certain reality, a certain truth. And what is true is always good, whether it's beautiful or dark, healing or painful, pleasing or disgusting. Truth is always a beacon, a guiding light pointing us back to the shore where our resiliency lies.

In writing and sharing stories, we humans are searching for hope; we're trying to make sense of our world by rejecting what's false, unwittingly searching for what's real and true, however small. We're reaching for something better, something beyond the suffering we feel in the here and now.

With all that being said, I've determined that writing *is* important. Words and stories offer more than "roses and rainbows." They're humanity's heart connection. Sharing them offers insight necessary for healing our individual and collective wounds and is critical in shaping our post-COVID world—a world where truth, hope, and resilience will prevail.

So, I'll join others who choose to write, knowing our words are important, for they offer resilience and comfort for a re-imagined yet undetermined future beyond COVID and 2020. They're beacons of truth and hope, guiding us as we navigate the tumultuous seas ahead.

LEANING INTO TOMORROW AFTER COVID

Jan Marquart

I take a cautious breath leaning into an unknown future after nearly two years of COVID chaos. I've already been duped by thinking the vaccinations had given me wings. They didn't. With the Delta variant upon us and on the rise, I am back in my world of isolated survival. It is difficult to understand why some resist the answer of being vaccinated to save lives.

People ask me how I am surviving being isolated. As a single woman, I am not isolated. I am in solitary confinement. Although I would like to say that being in such confinement has given me time to write, make better carrot soup, learn to speak Spanish, it has not. I am used to a lot of alone time and I have creative projects to keep me busy, but I found myself fatigued and trying to rest from the relentless bombardment of continued negative news. My psychotherapy practice filled with acute stress disorders and anxiety the likes of which I have never seen in my 53 years of service.

I have had to switch my perspective on how to make peace with such trauma. I didn't have the luxury of letting the situation get to me. I had to find a way. I resorted to prayer, rest, meditation when I could find time to untangle myself, and read books on how to care for the soul. My country was soul sick. I was soul sick. I have an entire shelf of books on how to care for the soul. I devoured them one after the other.

It was sad to hear that people were losing trust in their community members because they refused to take the pandemic and its suffering seriously. Clients asked me how we could change the consciousness of neighbors and family who risk spreading the virus. A woman without a mask in a dollar store tried to convince me that COVID is a hoax by the Democrats. It left me in a state of shock and disbelief that anyone in America could think such a reality was possible, let alone logical. I left the store so baffled and frightened I was shaking.

I don't have a clear vision of what leaning forward would look like. I just find myself in constant prayer that we as individuals and a nation will find a way to move on with more grace than has been displayed in the last year-and-a-half. We must bridge the gaps of the masked and unmasked, the vaccinated and the unvaccinated, to attain a sense of unity. All I can do is my part, my one and tiny part.

In the '70s, I read that one positive thought negates one thousand negative thoughts. I don't know how to prove or disprove that point, but I love thinking that just one of my thoughts can help the planet in such a simple way. Wasn't it Gandhi who said that you should be the change you want to see?

My life has not been void of suffering and sudden tragedies. I have had my share. But this pandemic, and its effect on my life, has been different. This time it was an experience of not just me in my own little life, suffering my own personal Job and Joseph losses, but of hearing and watching it play out in the world. This time I sat in suffering with my neighbors, community, town, state, country, and yes, through no exaggeration, the world. I have learned to come back to being mindful many times a day, to center on keeping my thoughts, prayers, and energy positive.

Every relationship is a commitment. If it doesn't hurt to wear a mask for the health and safety of others, just do it. Why not? We eat all kinds of chemicals. We have sprayed Lysol prolifically and Lysol is toxic. Read the darn label. But no one stops to question that, and you breathe that in as long as the particulates stay in the air in your home. You eat food with colored dyes in it. For goodness sake, people started taking horse pills that had nothing to do with viruses. You don't have to love the government, but the government has many good people in it working to keep our food, air, water, and medical world safe. Are they perfect? No. But we count on them without knowing it in many ways. Do I like taking meds – a big resounding NO. I concentrate on being as natural and organic as I can in everything I do, wear, eat, and buy. But taking care of each other is the right thing to do. It is the thing to do that builds our character and integrity. It is the thing to do to keep our hearts mindful and kind. It is the right thing to do. No exceptions, no excuses, no declarations of standing on the ground of freedom. What is so free about doing stupid things so you can be self-righteous? If the government didn't come up with vaccines, what would people do then? Wouldn't they hold them accountable? Which way do you want it? It has been a struggle not to get into my own mental battles on this issue. This has seemed to take far too much of my energy. I have had to deal with my process anew.

Thank God for the trees outside my study's window, that kept bringing me back to center with their indefatigable strength. They have seen and endured many storms. How did they do it? They have stood against fierce winds, survived unmovable Texas heat, and remained standing strong when the soil became too wet from our spring storms. I listened to their stillness and tried to extract their fortitude. I made the following plan for my tiny part of all this madness, to go forward without losing my mind:

I don't want to take the dead and dark mindsets of others with me into tomorrow.

I want to make beauty from ashes, from the personal and private lessons I have learned. That is where my personal power lies.

I have dropped my cholesterol 30 points by enjoying my own cooking rather than eating out. I'll continue this regimen.

I realized I do not need weekly trips to buy unneeded items at Target and TJ Maxx.

I will continue to send warm thoughts and inspiration to friends by writing cards, letting them know they are remembered and letting myself realize I am not alone.

I like nesting and want to continue investing in my home as a sacred place for healing myself through meditation for the world and myself.

I've made lists of people who have done me harm in thought, word, and deed, and I have slept better after praying for their wellbeing and healing, sending them forgiveness and pink arrows of joy right before I turn off the lights.

I love being in my kitchen creating new recipes and often do so in the middle of the night after frustrating conversations with those who still believe the pandemic is a hoax instead of the catastrophic situation it is.

I want to remember that wherever I go and whatever happens in the world I can thrive through it all with grace, forgiveness, and right action.

I have tucked the oldest tree outside my window into my heart. I rest with it, God's grace, and remain in prayer. It is the only way I have found to be truly well in such troubling times.

If we don't all go forward with the voice of caring for each other, making sure our personal tiny part of the world is kind and loving, what are we doing?

Perhaps that is the best place to start, for now.

NO FINAL LIST

Hudson Sierra

at the beginning of the pandemic
when I was 14 years old
I made a list of things I wanted to do before I turned 16
because in my 14-year-old head
that's as far as I could see into the future
normal teenage things like
go ride a scooter downtown
try Dunkin donuts
eat a kinder egg
dye my hair purple
get a car
and other not-so-normal things that suit me like
see a drag show
do goat yoga
get a tarot reading
speak to the dead
after I turned 15, I had to make a new to-do list
a list of not-so-fun entertaining tasks
like love myself
eat out with my friends anywhere we want
don't go to the bathroom after every meal
stop looking at the scissors like that
not check a label on that candy wrapper
make midnight toast and not cry about it
take a shower and not have my hair fall out
these were hard to-do's
and by the time I finally hit 16
I had checked off all of those things
and I can make a new list
because I know I will make it further than
14-year-old me thought I could

MY NEXT TWENTY YEARS

Christy Piszkiewicz

My son-in-law, Brian, brought so much love with him when he married my daughter, Allison. His parents, Ann and Jerry, were friends my husband and I would have picked even if our children had not brought us together.

Our families were together for dinner, and Ann told me she wanted to show me something. A photo on her phone showed Millie, her mother, in a striped bathing suit jumping in the waves. I gasped when Ann told me it was taken twenty years ago, when her mom was sixty-five.

Looking over to the couch where Milly was sitting, we gazed at her. She was frail, gray, and even though her mind was sharp, she needed the walker to get around. She also tired quickly.

I could hear my breath as I exhaled. I had just turned 66 last December, and while I was not as quick as I once was, I still considered myself reasonably healthy.

My mother had died at 70 of heart problems.

After we drove the short distance home from Allie and Brian's house, my husband, Paul, must have seen a crazy look in my eye, for he handed me a gin and tonic.

Pulling a photo album from the shelf, I went through pictures until I got to our daughter's birth pictures.

"Here's my mom at 64," I stated as I showed Paul the book. "She looks just like me now."

"Yes, I do see the resemblance. It's your mother, for gosh sake, but honey, you're young and nothing like your mom. You've always been active."

"So was my mom. Remember the baby shower she threw? How she took care of Allie when I was still working?"

A concerned but understanding look came over his face. He realized what I was trying to say. Taking hold of his hand, which always fits nicely in mine, I continued, "The next twenty years are OUR years, hon. We have to make the best of them, now."

A smile filled his face, and he laughed. "Twenty years felt like a life sentence when the kids were small!"

In the next few months, we started to plan. Travel to Seattle to see our son, time in New Mexico, and a trip to Poland. I always wanted to know the land of my grandparents. It was time for us to splurge.

Then the Covid Pandemic put all our big travel plans on hold. So we found other ways to enjoy our "next twenty years."

We purchased a red fishing boat, small enough that our car could tow it but big enough to hold us and, when the isolation was over, our two grandchildren.

The fishing boat was a marvelous way to relax on a nearby lake. Caesar's Creek Lake was close enough to be in the water in twenty minutes. (Took a lot longer going home—do you have any idea how hard it is to back up a boat trailer in a boat slip?)

It was so invigorating in the spring to see the water come back after a cold winter, as the shoreline went from a colorless gray to bright green dabs growing everywhere. Summer's sun was glistening on the water as we saw eagles fly over; that was magical. Autumn's gold, red and orange colors enchanted us as a couple during cooler temperatures.

On days that were too hot or rainy (this is Ohio), enjoying leisurely lunches while watching the birds at the feeders, inventing zucchini recipes for our bounteous harvest, or binge-watching shows, we still relished our days.

Zooming relatives and making up funny "Top 10 Reasons" why we loved the birthday person found us being surprisingly creative.

We came to live in a jungle, for we loved planting and watering but hated weeding.

Finally, we received the vaccines.

As the Pandemic restrictions started to ease, we came to a new realization. We still wanted to travel and see different places, but doing even little things together developed the accurate "snapshot" of our next twenty years.

MORE OF THE SAME...PLEASE

Debra Dolan

Prior to the global pandemic, I had been living a very quiet, uncomplicated, and simple life, healing from injuries sustained in a seemingly innocuous accident in 2015. As I focused on recovering from post-concussion syndrome, vestibular issues, and damage to occipital nerves, I found myself on a mandatory retreat in my own home and neighbourhood. Healing required drastically limiting social interactions; maintaining physical distance as people often appeared closer than they actually were; avoiding hugs and handshakes in order to preserve energy; the loss of gainful employment; reducing trips to the grocery store due to crowds, sound, and light; and no longer being able to participate in community writing or exercise programs. After decades of an interesting life filled with fascinating people and activities, I found myself in lockdown as my daily routines and movements were altered without choice. I was cut off from the city, employment, and those I cared about most.

During the initial period of adjustment, I used to hide my intense feelings from others because I feared they would not understand. Unfortunately, now they do, due to COVID-19 and the many restrictions on personal freedom and the risks to financial security since March 2020. Life as they have known it will never be the same either. As my friends, neighbours, and family members experience unprecedented changes to their lives, I can offer comfort and awareness of what many people, such as myself, have experienced for years and learned to accommodate, as well as thrive. They were surprised to learn of the similarities as they acclimated these past 18 months, viewing my situation through a different lens. There was a time when I, too, was concerned about losing employment, home, friendships, finances, and well-being. I was lonely because I could not leave my apartment freely. In addition, I was scared, discovering there was no cure for the pain I was experiencing and that specialists might not be able to help me. I had to learn to slow down, relax, take intentional life-enhancing breaths, trust, and interact with others more creatively in order to remain connected. I was forced to ration energy, resources, and expectations, and I leaned into acceptance. Concurrently, there was an involuntary compulsion to think deeply about my life and choices. I missed so much and yet as my world shrank further into solitude it also expanded in unexpected ways. I had a renewed appreciation for the home I had created. I was grateful for my life-long passions: reading, writing, and solitary walking. I was thankful I had experience with living alone. I had time, which had seemed elusive during many, many years.

It feels oddly strange to admit that I have enjoyed it so much. I have, actually. As the world closed in March 2020, I simultaneously started to feel more alive, normalized, and hopeful. These personal, small, incremental gains continue in my life as the world prepares for reopening. I hope I do not experience a setback.

I no longer feel as alone. I am no longer striving to do what everyone else is doing. I am no longer missing—during COVID-19 my social interactions have dramatically increased, as others virtually reach out through various technologies and the internet responds to new ways of participating in life's offerings. I used to believe that the intranet provided a false sense of intimacy; now, I am appreciating its manifold gifts. I also appreciate my small 'bubble' of close friends.

As my own recovery has naturally progressed, so have the advances in COVID-19 vaccination creation, procurement, distribution, and inoculation. I see how far I have come in accommodating my 'normal' as others discern theirs. I hear of them going through the stages, as after a bit of Netflix binging, they discover there is more they want to do with the empty time laid before them. There is an opportunity to tackle the projects or self-improvement ideas they have been ruminating. Some are meditating for the first time; others are crafting, learning to play guitar or a new language, baking. The internet has exploded with lovely concerts, podcasts, church services, museum and art gallery tours. From the comfort of your own home, you can now watch Bolshoi Ballet, National Theatre Live, and new cinematic releases.

I spoke with a friend recently who after years finally had the time and inclination to do a closet purge. Like many people, she owns more stuff than she can actually use or need. I shared a similar exercise I had completed two years before, when I was accepted into long-term disability and realized that I would not be returning to the downtown office where I had worked. I found a large cardboard box and, with the same efficiency my friend described, I packed for donation all the business clothes I no longer identified with or had not worn for two winters. I spread them all over the bed and the floor. Skirt suits and trouser suits, coats, shoes, bags, scarves and coats, and all, I am proud to write, immaculately kept. There were no descending hems or missed buttons and all items were freshly washed or dry-cleaned awaiting recovery. As I placed them into their new temporary home, I felt elated knowing another woman will have the same sense of independence and confidence that I had experienced wearing them.

I have witnessed the benefits of time and patience, advocacy, self-care, limiting life's pleasures, and listening carefully to medical practitioners' expertise in clearing a path for future living. I can see my old self before me, filled with energy, compassion, and kind enthusiasm, and I hope to fully embrace her acquaintance once again. This feels like the intersection of going forward and not back in recovery, the place where I trust when to rest and when to push myself as I understand fully the benefits of both. I am awakened by the collective vulnerability as each individual discovers for themselves what to keep and what to throw away, determining what really matters in these unprecedented times. History informs us that one day COVID-19 and its many variants will not be in the driver's seat of our lives.

As I ruminate about what may lay ahead, it is suddenly apparent that life is closer to ending than beginning. Two questions constantly surface: "*If not now…when?*" and "*Am I living my best life?*" No more excuses. No more wasted time or waiting. I am examining my dreams, as I have no greater fear than missed opportunities and experiences. A core belief is that regret is not about what I do, but rather what I didn't. My choices now are not only inspired by what I want for myself, but also by how I want to be remembered: a role model of a strong person with an independent life, who lived and loved on her own terms.

Finding Community

STRANGERS ON A PLANE, SHARING

Len Leatherwood

On a recent plane flight from LA to Dallas, I sat in the window seat and had two young men in the seats next to me. We were all masked per federal rules and, unlike most trips when I say only a cursory hello to my seatmates, we fell into immediate conversation. Over the next two hours and thirty minutes, we each shared details about our lives: our work, passions, and activities that brought us joy. We also talked about how Covid had affected us. One young man was Jewish and the other Latino, and there I was, old enough to be at least their mother and perhaps even their grandmother.

These young men couldn't have been more open, kind, attentive, and generous to me and to each other. Each shared, listened, and kept moving the conversation deeper and deeper. Before it was over, I knew that one was ready for a career change and the other was viewing the world from a more open spiritual perspective. I assured the one young man not to sell his intellect short. He was clearly bright and had all sorts of options he could consider. As for the other, we agreed that religion could be broader than orthodoxy and that living a life motivated by love was the key.

When we were leaving at the end of the flight, we stepped into the airport and stopped. One young man said, "Wow, I've just made two great friends and now we have to say goodbye." We didn't hug because of Covid, but we exchanged Facebook information with each other. We promised we'd see each other online. Since that time, they have indeed sent friend requests and I've accepted.

How lucky for me to stumble upon these two sterling examples of youth, each grappling with life in his own way and being willing to share some of those challenges with two strangers. Without Covid-19 and its isolation, I'm not sure that conversation ever would have happened. We were, after all, three people starved for connection with others from the outside world.

What a joyful experience that was! I hope to watch on Facebook as their lives move forward. Both deserve the very best that life can bring. They clearly are ready to share their kindness and decency with the world. How fortunate for me that on that particular day, I was the lucky recipient of their time, and was treated as a friend.

ONE LITTLE BOY IN BLUE

Lin M. Brummels

"And the cat's in the cradle and the silver spoon
Little boy blue and the man in the moon"
— HARRY CHAPIN

People gather on the grass by the lake for music in the park
as afternoon mist moves east, overcast skies clear just in time.

Music is planned for every other week now after Covid
cancelled most events last summer. After a year

quarantined, children run uphill and down, turn
cartwheels and dance with abandon while the band plays.

One little boy in blue, about two, repeatedly runs circles
around his mother on the grass a few feet ahead of us.

His determined face is a study in childhood, as his energy
entices older, bigger kids to let him play with them,

regularly spinning back to mother for a hug. He reaches
out to others and his smile invites us to share his joy.

BUILD A CASTLE

Claire Butler

Intolerance and public shaming have given rise to a new term that has entered the vernacular: cancel culture.

In the first weeks of 2020, at about the same time COVID-19 took its hold on America, a new phenomenon was growing in popularity. It began in 2019 with an interview given by Kanye West to Michael Barbaro of *The New York Times'* "The Daily," wherein West said he was being "canceled" because of his support of Donald Trump. He repeated that sentiment throughout the interview. Thus was born "cancel culture." It is the withdrawal of support for and acknowledgment of another person's existence in response to an opinion that he or she advances that is antithetical to the other's beliefs—and it's gaining momentum.

What happened to the ages-old, polite way of entering into dialogue with someone and getting to the bottom of things before simply writing them off? Is cancel culture leading us down a path of "we must be the same and think the same?" If so, that would be a shame because different thinking is what invented so many wonderful life treasures like the telephone and the internet—two things invented to bring people together.

It is my hope that life after COVID wakes us up to the importance of people regardless of their beliefs. That we can return to an earlier era when people appreciated another's position and could learn something. I look forward to smiles and pleasantries amongst strangers passing each other on the street. I'd like to see us regain our enthusiasm for travel, and experience safety in all respects, including plain, old-fashioned conversation. If necessary, leave touchy matters alone. Find a common interest and talk about that without judgment. Cancel out "cancel culture."

A YouTube video filmed by Soul Pancake in 2013 in an undisclosed city brought strangers together in a ball pit. A pit was erected on a random busy street corner with a big sign: "Jump in, make a friend and find your 'common.'" There were no other instructions—no signs that dictated age, ethnicity, gender or faith. It offered a pure and simple opportunity for strangers to learn about each other.

There were several inflated balloons floating on top of the balls in the pit and on each balloon was written a question they might consider discussing. The questions were innocuous such as, "Name three things on your bucket list." Those questions led to conversation, laughter and, in some cases, empathy. Before parting ways, some created a unique handshake, took photos together on their phones, or hugged: they had made new friends.

My wish is for people to come together as if we lived in a giant ball pit. Division spreads rapidly from the do's and don'ts of COVID and the rights and wrongs of politics, pulling us apart one brain cell at a time. Nothing is ever achieved by drawing a line in the sand. Can't we instead sweep that sand into a big pile and build a castle…together?

UNSCHEDULED DESTINY

Jamuna Advani

A walk around the creek
a habit to enjoy,
the beauty of nature,
a gift to human life,
continues.
Pleasure looms from my heart
watching the soft dew glitter
on the green grass life span
before the rising sun
consumes its glitter of life.
While covid thunders around us
with alarming danger,
walk still goes on as usual,
while smiles hidden behind the masks
are a part of our greetings.
Coming across new friends
my heart dances tempestuously
as happiness blossoms.
Acknowledged smile exists forever.
While our friendship develops
more, closer than ever, now
gathered in the tiny corner of our sanity,
to be preserved beyond the covid era.

Threaded

Christina M. Wells

Some months back, my friend Clarissa gave me a small thread-art piece with white edges around the side and a purple butterfly in the center. She made it after hearing a family story I had both told her and written about in an essay. It meant a lot that she remembered its significance. It also strangely reminded me of thread art that had hung in my grandparents' living room when I was small, something she couldn't possibly have known about, unless she had filed it in her subconscious after seeing a picture of my cousin and me in front of it, legs dangling halfway to the floor. She seemed not to remember seeing the photo, at all.

Earlier in the pandemic, every evening around the same time, Clarissa silently texted me because of some things that were going on in her life. There was no eyeroll, no passive aggressive threat that she text me so I wouldn't call to track her down. She simply sent a note each evening, once remarking, "It's kind of nice we've been able to check in at the same time every day."

I learned what it was like for her to begin graduate school at her own computer. We had celebrated her graduation from college and her graduate school plans, and I had thought about how proud of her I was and how much I looked forward to sitting at her graduation, even as some people would have dreaded sitting outside in Charlottesville in May, baking beside all the caps and gowns. It was a sunny day when I optimistically had this thought and, let's face it, it's the sunny days we look back on, dumbfounded by our own surprise.

There was no graduation ceremony, at least not then. I celebrated her degree, her internship, her new job, and every other thing that managed to lift up a time when things seemed to happen slowly. Something like relief happens when someone young tells you that they had a good day, even though it happened quietly through screens.

Some of us mother differently. Some of us don't exactly mother, at all.

She is not my daughter, though sometimes I think the nebulous air of daughter-sister-niece-friend hangs over us somewhere, like the plaque I gave her about friends who are family, and the soundtrack of her playing the cello that she gave me when I was looking for meditation music in the middle of a global pandemic. I have listened to her say many things, and she, too, has listened.

I don't call myself a mentor because I don't like to think of myself as a dispenser of knowledge, someone telling her how to be. Besides, what did I know when she talked about an ex-boyfriend, a profession that wasn't mine, and a choice of jobs that I never had to make? All of her stories were so different from mine, and the difference was equalizing.

At one point I sat in a Zoom room mostly filled with mothers who offered information about their children in their introductions. This is the ID that gets exchanged to say: this is my life. That's yours. *How many do you have? These are the names of mine. Mine are in school; mine have impacted my life this way. I might have screwed mine up this other way. Oh, thanks for saying you think I'm not a bad mother.* I have no particular right to any of those words, nothing to say that from birth forward, I have taken care of little people, feeding them and watering them, making them grow. What I do know is that while some of these women desperately needed to get their kids out of the house, I looked forward to the point in the pandemic when I could finally hang out with someone else's adult child, a kid I didn't raise who somehow ended up in my life.

I have sometimes liked the idea of being a clean-up crew for people who need or want extra adults to tell them that they are okay, or that they are extraordinary, really, whether their parents say so or not. There are no obvious cultural expectations, perhaps, and maybe we should make some up to make it real enough when people talk about their families, and we want ours to count.

I imagine that at the start of the pandemic, people sometimes bent the rules with their own adult kids, figuring out ways that they could be under one roof without creating a super-spreader event worthy of a CDC report with the names redacted. I erred on the side of caution until a sunny day in the seventies, when Clarissa was in town and we planned to go to a park, even though we'd never been to a park together before. I picked one she thought she had gone to once in fifth grade with her class, and she knew where it was. It's near my family's house, and it's near her parents' house. There's a large field, and there's a branch of the Cross County Trail running through historic land crossed by troops in the Civil War. It's always interesting to think about how it now connects one town or suburb to another. If we all had to walk to friends without getting in the street much, we sort of could.

But we walked together, this non-daughter/non-sister and me. It was strange to see each other after a year, though we had talked often, and she doesn't live far away. Her parents are one suburb over, and the college she attended when I taught her is close by. There are many places nearby where people have typically gone, for varying degrees of connection and exchange. They mostly involve windows and doors.

It means something to meet someone, when you've more or less not left the house for a year, and you've turned down invitations to do other things. That day in the park, we walked looping trails, dodging bikes and moving over for unmasked walkers and their errant dogs. Later we sat at a picnic table by a skate park, under a leafless tree, and watched people find new ways to defy death, as if we hadn't watched that all year. There were moments of quiet as the wind shifted and the sun started to set, like it was an ordinary day and we still both went places all the time and just happened to pick a park that day. It felt to me like we once marked time silently somewhere far away, and now had marked it at another location, beside a creek and some very old trees.

Eventually, within a few months, we would be more typical, sitting in a restaurant, unmasked. I thought about that lunch as a different field trip from taking someone to lunch because they had graduated from college or applied for graduate programs. It was the same person. We're the same people, theoretically. Only we had talked at much greater distance in a pandemic, making us seem paradoxically a whole lot closer. We aren't family, yet we are. When you go to the trouble to see people when there's a Delta variant, you know that you care. That might say something positive of all this mess we've endured. We've learned our social habits.

Perhaps some connecting family threads are so invisible that we, ourselves, don't know exactly where they are or why we have them. Not everyone needs to know the threads are there for us to get that we link to everyone we've ever been, everyone we're close to, and perhaps, to everything that happens on the other side of an afternoon in the park with a young person—or much later in a long pandemic, with no masks holding us back. We can hold those connections no matter what happens next.

EMERGENCE

Patricia E. Eagle

At last, partial emergence
From the occurrence
Of COVID observance
That struck with a vengeance
And unfortunate cadence,

Demanding compliance
And a willingness to give credence
While exhibiting deference
To scientists of excellence
Unwilling to submit to submergence.

But for there to be coexistence
With an appropriate coalescence
We've been asked to stay aware of evidence
And make way for coherence
To vaccines and hygiene dependence.

Despite the dissidence
Of a former Prez with hot-headed flatulence
Confident of his eloquence
Regardless of incoherence
And a lack of competence,

Convinced of his eminence
While demonstrating ambivalence
Toward any benevolence or compassionate condolence,
Unwilling to guide us toward deterrence
In a pandemic screaming expedience!

Is it a coincidence?
This experience has no equivalence
And asks for a certain abstinence
From the debilitating incongruence
Of Black Lives Matter and White *a-f*-fluence.

Please, let's not have more divergence
But carefully consider how all this disturbance
Begs for necessary convergence.

Consider the consequence
Of avoiding concurrence
Refusing to admit the purpose of insurgents
Who overlooked our country's essence
And a new administration's attempts for a better existence
Who has asked for purposeful diligence
Wary of recurrence
And not wanting a resurgence.

When will we be ready to commence
To engage fully with emergence
Finally making changes with these issues of importance
Becoming a country illuminated by brilliance?

THE POWER OF HOPE

Nirmala Kshatriya

It was the night of March 9, 2020. I was all prepared to catch a flight the next morning for India. Having lived with my children in California for over a year-and-a-half, I missed Bangalore terribly. Early the next morning, my elder son called me and said, "Ma, I have to cancel your tickets." I thought he was joking because he knew how excited I was to go to India. He said he was concerned about this virus called the coronavirus that was spreading in China and Europe at that time. At my resistance, he suggested we delay the travel by a month to allow the virus to dissipate.

So I kept my bags packed hoping that the virus would disappear in a month's time and it would be safe for me to travel to my home in India.

Little did I know that my dream to spend blissful time with my brother and sisters in India would be replaced by eighteen months of lockdown filled with surprises, separations, new forms of connections, unexpected discoveries, simple joys, and a brand new normal. Slowly I accepted all of this as my normal way of life. My bags were unpacked; the chocolates that I bought for my seventy-year-old younger brother were stored on the upper shelves of my room and other packets of gifts were also kept safe. I was thinking that I would be going home in a couple of months anyway. But my journey was not meant to be. I am still living in California in the company of my grandchildren.

Now all the new norms – like masks, social distancing, Zoom calls, virtual hugs, and virtual parties are accepted wholeheartedly. Some of the changes that the pandemic has brought about and around our lives are likely going to stay permanently, whether we like it or not.

The pandemic appeared to cause a struggling economy, but objectively, business *models* are struggling rather than business itself. Consider for example the food industry – restaurants were almost empty during lockdown but home delivery services did business like never before. The automobile sector, which is often a pointer to the economy, is supposed to have taken a beating. Fewer cars were purchased, but ride-share services like Uber and Lyft grew.

Basic human values came to the surface – like empathy, kindness, caring, and helping others. We have learned that life can be lived simply, and that kind of life is quite happy and peaceful! One more thing I noticed: we are more aware about our health by being more disciplined in exercising, practicing yoga, and meditation.

The IT industry saw a new trend called 'work from home' that showed phenomenal savings on the cost of infrastructure. The list of savings will be very long, the individual outputs in terms of quality and quantity being very high. Similarly, the concept of teaching online has turned into a reality. It is an enormous change in the traditional culture of teaching, a totally new experience altogether.

If we examine it deeply, there is no change in the basic transaction of materials, but there are radical changes in transactional modes. That is my reading of the outer world.

My inner world is full of peace and joy. My little grandchildren are growing up, and I see them turning into good humans, going to college and doing well. I love to watch how they feel about their friends and neighbors, and the goodwill and respect they have for everything around them. It makes me feel so hopeful about the future – what more could one want? My youngest grandchildren are toddlers now. I don't have to do a Zoom call with them anymore. I just go to their house now and the two-year-old comes running to me and starts telling some stories in his babbling language. I now can understand what he wants to say, like if he has gone to see a train, which he calls tan-tan, or he saw the moon in the sky, which is Bmoony [full moon] or Lemony [little moony].

One of the biggest reasons why I was missing my town – Bangalore in India – was that I was missing my neighbors and my friends. I used to meet them almost every evening. But slowly I came to know the friends of my children and their parents, and we have all become close. I now have groups of friends. We meet in parks or in backyards, with masks on and with social distancing, and it's so much fun. Life seems to be perfect – in a strange way, that's thanks to the lockdown.

So at the twilight of my life, I feel so fulfilled, so assured that friendships, love, gratitude, and all other human values will survive, even in hard or difficult times. The power of the human spirit is invincible.

INTERCONNECTEDNESS

Sandra Stanko

The path was slippery with mud and decaying leaves. My heartbeat had been skipping and skittering up my esophagus and settling in the back of my throat, making me feel as if I were choking. I felt sporadic waves of dizziness. These ailments—instigated by the pandemic madness— were my reason for seeking out this path on this particular day here in the Appalachian foothills in Western Pennsylvania. It was March 2020.

The path was called the "Discovery Trail" and wound through Appalachian woods on a ridge of the Allegheny Mountains. The trail was punctuated by numbered plaques displaying nature-themed poems by famous and local writers. As I ambled over the uneven ground, stepping over logs and sliding on underbrush, I breathed in the woodsy air and absorbed the verses. Robert Frost's familiar words urged me to take the road "less traveled by." Professor Gian Pagnucci piqued my interest in locating a "water stone," which is "charcoal gray except for one white chip" that he had carried from Lake Superior and left here for me to find. Vietnam veteran and Appalachian poet Ronald Smits identified boulders as "whale-rocks" and contemplated their riding the "wave-ridges" of the

Appalachians to this, their final resting spot. As I stood on one of Smits' whale-rocks and looked north across the hollow, breathing deeply of the forest, my heart rate dropped to a normal rhythm. I felt a peace that belied the uncertain chaos in the world. Here in these woods, fear felt far away. Here, the trees continued to stretch heavenward, the birds continued to chirp and sing, and those whale-rocks remained stationary after their long, prehistoric journey. Here was calmness—and peace.

Interconnected Patterns of Order

Nature doesn't like chaos. It is always working to regain or maintain a balanced state. The tornado forms because of the instability of the air; the funnel serves as a restructuring of the opposing forces of temperature, air pressure, and wind. Forests of trees are interconnected deep within the ground, their roots joining in a mutually beneficial system of physical and communicative support. And into the chaos of my pandemic-infused, anxiety-ridden environment, nature intervened as a force of stability, a salve to my mental and emotional fragileness. In spite of what was happening in the outward, tumultuous world, nature was there for the inner me. As more and more places for interaction were taken away, the natural world opened even more, like a blooming flower that I had just recognized was there all along, its dewy pinkness and tender leaves held out to me, beckoning me to be a part of its unfolding.

Inner Truth

My outward experiences touched the inklings of a deeper inner truth. I journaled. I reflected. I meditated. And my mind was drawn to that original Garden of Eden, described as being an abundant place planted by the Creator. [1] Where the word "creation" implies making something out of nothing, "planting" implies deliberate, loving, and nurturing efforts for intended and expected growth. In this garden were beautiful trees that produced delicious fruit and at the center of the garden were the tree of life and the tree of the knowledge of good and evil. [2]

Then an unexpected insight emerged. In this garden, the trees, flowers, animals, water, and people were words, everything flowing beautifully together, in interconnected patterns and natural harmony. The tree of life and the tree of the knowledge of good and evil comprised the thesis—the main part around which everything else in the garden was anchored.

What an interesting concept! Not only can words be used to describe a garden, but also the garden itself can be thought of as being words. The garden is bigger than just its flora and fauna in being a tapestry of sounds and letters, deliberately planted and thus purposefully written. That idea can be transposed to all of nature. Planting is a writing of sorts, with the words of nature being written throughout the innumerable sensory textures and patterns of the natural world, including the feathers and songs of the birds, the scales and fins of the fish, the rivers, the leaves and seeds of the trees, and even those moss-covered whale-rocks. Poignantly, the Greek translation of "pattern" is *prótypo*, which is also the basis for the English words "type" and "typology"—writing! The interrelationship of language mirrors the connected patterns in all of nature, including flora, fauna, and people living within the effects of a worldwide pandemic.

The Return

I returned to the Discovery Trail in February 2021. As I walked, I noticed that the trees were brown and brittle from the dormant season, it being much too early for greens. Or so I thought. As I rounded a corner heading south on the path, I glimpsed a lush green groundcover that was spread before me through the shady underbrush. I was able to identify the plant with clusters of oval, gently serrated leaves as Japanese pachysandra, an evergreen shrub that is native to Japan but had been introduced to eastern North America. The low-to-the-ground, bright green leaf clusters, absent of the small white flowers that the plant would produce in the spring, were a shocking contrast against all of the browns and darks of the winter woods. It seemed meaningful as well that my name was embedded into the name of this evergreen. It made me a part of this resilience, a plant that stayed true to its original color even amidst the seasonal, worldly changes around it. I could be that resilient, too.

Collective Hope

I had, in fact, made a crucial discovery while walking on the Appalachian Discovery Trail. While the pandemic has been a time of fear and panic, order is prevailing, and I tapped into one of those ordering forces, the natural world itself. As worldly chaos has unfolded, the trees have persisted in their growth, the birds have continued to chortle and warble, and those whale-rocks have remained standing as prehistoric sentinels, perpetually gazing across the hallow at evidence of the natural cycles of seasonal growth and rebirth, echoing from ridge to ridge and throughout time.

I realized another important lesson: the balance that is reflected in nature can be mine in a symbiotic, mutually beneficial relationship with nature itself. I have to give as much as take. In the exchange of breathing in the phytoncides from the trees that can help me to feel calmer, I release carbon dioxide for those same trees' absorption. While I walk through the forest, I have to respect that I am walking in another's home. When my senses take in a plethora of smells and sounds, I have to express gratitude.

The pandemic time has brought me a new appreciation of not only this interconnectedness and symbiosis but also agency. While so much of this volatile time has felt out of control, my experiences in nature reaffirmed a sense of control and resilience like my namesake, the Japanese pachysandra. I am the tree of life and the tree of the knowledge of good and evil, the thesis of my ongoing story. I am the cog in the center of the wheel, touching the spokes of these life-altering lessons:

- We are all intertwined and interdependent, a complex network of roots and branches, feelings and experiences, hands and hearts.
- We are symbiotic, giving and taking in a delicate dance of balance.
- Each of us embodies the thesis of our own ongoing story.
- We each have inner wisdom and must trust ourselves enough to tap into it.
- We each have the ability to sustain our resilience, even through difficult times.

These are my visions for a new, post-pandemic world, a world with agency and reliance, a world with mutual embracing, a world with inner power, hope, and peace. And nature will be our continuing guide and model, if we are just open to listening.

A Course in Miracles says, "The miracle but calls your ancient Name, which you will recognize because the truth is in your memory." [3] The truth lives inside all of us. And it lives in nature. In today's uncertainty, that knowledge and acknowledgement can make all of the difference.

[1] Genesis 2:8
[2] Genesis 2:9
[3] T-26. VII.16:1, *A Course in Miracles*. 3rd ed., Foundation for Inner Peace 2007.

Building Resilience

COVID and Beyond
Claire Butler

"As Susan Wittig Albert noted, 'It often seems too many people find it easiest to believe that going forward means going back to the good times we had before.' But we've seen the division and injustice in our society, and we can't un-see it. How will our individual lives look when the world has recovered from COVID-19?"
— Susan Schoch

Recovering from COVID is going to be a journey, and going forward I think we should review the past. We need to learn from our errors and make adjustments in our lives for inclusivity and compassion for our fellow human beings. It's a perfect way to celebrate the end of the virus.

The past has given us good instruction for our future, if we choose to pay attention to it. At my age, I can recall the Fifties and Sixties. It was a time when crime was almost nonexistent; we left the doors to our homes unlocked even when away. In the Sixties, we jumped rope and held nightly kickball games in the street—all were invited to join in regardless of color or faith. Children PLAYED, not on computers or gaming devices, but REALLY played with each other, face-to-face. They got to know each other, and hence they cared about each other. I wonder if the decline of that type of social activity has affected, or infected, us with a different kind of virus: Alexithymia.

Alexithymia is not really a virus, but a medical diagnosis: "the inability to identify and express or describe one's feelings." Afflicted people lack social skills, empathy and emotion, including joy and love. Little is known about this condition, but it is believed that it can be environmental—so do our current preoccupations with technology, and our lack of face-to-face interaction with others, numb our feelings of empathy and compassion? COVID has taken us deeply into isolation.

We've now lived without sharing our smiling faces with friends, family and strangers for much longer than a year. Intolerance and crime have risen to unfathomable heights, and people are angry, just as they might be angry with high temperatures for weeks on end with no rain in sight, and they project that anger toward those they encounter.

How will we recover from the estrangement that COVID unleashed on us? Certainly recovery will be slow, thanks to our already busy lives with little time for contemplation. What about Zoom meetings? Have we become addicted to staying in our pajamas all day to conduct business? For too long, we've experienced reclusiveness that prevented us from learning, observing and caring. It invited us to bury our heads in the sand, "If it didn't happen to me, it doesn't apply to me." Crime, hate and racial discontent became daily expectations in the media. COVID is not solely responsible for that, but it has certainly exacerbated the situation for an already suffering nation. COVID is more than a virus; it is a deep, dark hole from which we must now climb out.

In the Sixties, we saw an extraordinary rise in color consciousness— and prejudice against any culture other than White Anglo-Saxon Protestant was acceptable in most social spheres. Dr. Martin Luther King, Jr. arrived on the scene, determined to make peace between the races. In response to his call for equality, he was assassinated. James Baldwin was so discouraged with American prejudice that he chose to leave his home in Harlem for the tranquility of the French countryside. In the land of the free, how does that make any sense? Why do we not learn?

During the past year, I have watched our society slowly implode. We've made little progress in our social responsibilities and compassion for others. Our world, and more specifically, The United States, is now a hotbed of crime and hate. Politics depressed us, the press tenaciously worked to guide our every thought, and the restraints of COVID made things worse as we sheltered in place, covering half our faces in public and standing six feet apart. Hate, road rage and disillusion became common experiences, and instead of coming together to fight the real enemy, we drew a line in the sand, chose sides, and focused on people rather than the circumstances that caused it. Our blame was and is misplaced.

Why is it that we must, as a nation, always have an enemy? And, if there is no "outside" enemy, we begin gnawing on our own feet. There is a book by Roger Fisher and William Ury that is decades old. *Getting to Yes* is a blueprint for negotiating differences between people to resolve unmovable issues. Its principles are often employed in lawsuits when litigants cannot agree. The idea is for everyone to come to the roundtable with an open mind, leaving positions and prejudices at the door. There are rules of conduct, and respect for others is key. They discuss matters openly, face-to-face, calmly and civilly, to reach an understanding or agreement. And it works. If I could afford to, I'd send a copy of that book to every representative in Washington, because they have become polarized in their thinking with no room for negotiation.

What would our lives be like if we did not automatically assume the worst about our fellow men and women, and instead opened the floodgates for Discussion rather than Destruction? A first step might be to embrace people for their differences. How boring our lives would be if we were all exactly the same and thought exactly the same. "Be kind in word and deed," my grandmother taught me. You just cannot go wrong with that.

So, what then is the answer to the question posed in the opening quote: "How will our individual lives look when the world has recovered from COVID-19?" We won't know what the future holds for us until we get there, but I hope every day that recovery will bring peace and understanding.

THE PANDEMIC

Patricia Roop Hollinger

I never thought I would be wearing a mask
As I went about my daily task

Why this was only done in faraway places
We Americans never covered our faces

Then CNN and MSNBC were talking about a pandemic
Is that something like an epidemic?

Governor Hogan said we must cover our faces
Even in the most remote places

Next was the shortage of toilet paper
Attempting to find some became quite a caper

No more gathering in the Bistro to eat
Finally, we had to admit defeat

Our apartment became our safe harbor
Why we couldn't even go to the barber!

Photo albums are now all updated
Some of old boyfriends I once dated.

For neighbors I baked something good to eat
I was not yet ready to admit defeat

'Cause staying in touch said, "I care."
When surrounded by a virus that gave us a scare

Now we are able to go out and eat
Reminding us how much that is a treat

There are those now who refuse vaccination
Something I did without any hesitation

We are fortunate we live in a nation
That can afford for all to have a vaccination

So, roll up your sleeve; and get it done
Then we can say the virus has not won

LEAN IN AND LIFT YOUR FEET

Merimée Moffitt

No car for me until it's electric, snappy, push-button, plug-in
No house downsizing until it makes sense to let mine go
Get undepressed, as in levitate, bubble up, do laughter yoga

take that trip, when you feel safe enough from the
unwashed, unvaxxed, unknowing. Learn again.
Get some new capris even if they're brand new. Feel good.
Make love. Don't miss a date with friends.
Be a friend. Make a date. Finish my book. Just do it.
Cook vegan and veggie and local. Eat what
I want and need and must and have, even if it's
Native local-grown meat, delicious prairie grass.
I have no desire to paint and draw or make anything
other than poems. It's time to piece together
the next book. Call it the last one, and be done.
Then the cruise in my all-electric car/camper
sleeper all for one. Or go trailer nomading
with the handy husband for good company.
Cut loose, Mama. There is life yet to be lived.

DIRECT DIAL

Joan Connor

Rrrrrrriiinnngggg!

Thank you for calling the Post-Covid Adjustment Information Center. If you know your party's extension you may dial it direct. If not, stay IN the line and you will be helped in the order of your call. Waiting time is currently one lifetime.

The directory is as follows. Listen carefully. Several extensions have changed or been removed due to the new variants upon the Covid scene, in addition to the original virus. Please be aware that mandates are just that! Dates change according to man.

Dial:
#1 to reach the Department of Optimism
#2 to reach the Department of Pessimism
#3 to reach the Department of the Masked
#4 to reach the Department of the Unmasked
#5 to reach the Department of the Vaccinated

#6 to reach the Department of the Unvaccinated
#7 to reach the Department of Cards Required to Enter
#8 to reach the Department of No Card Required

Rrrrrrriiinnnggg! Rrrrrrriiinnnggg! Rrrrrrriiinnnggg! Rrrrrrriiinnnggg! Rrrrrrriiinnnggg!

#1 Sorry, but the Department of Optimism has closed early for the day, for the month, for the year, for the decade. Please have your call transferred to Extension #2.

#2 You have reached the Department of Pessimism. All lines are busy, but you can receive a call back in approximately 24 hours, well, maybe 48 hours, no, let's make that next month. We have been taking as many calls each day as possible. They are increasing in droves. Perhaps, you can have your call transferred to the Bureau of Doom and Gloom.

#3 Thank you for calling the Department of the Masked. We are happy to help you, but our agents are currently out of the office collecting data to determine the percentage of folks dedicated to protecting others as they breathe. Yes, our agents are in and out.

#4 You have been connected to the Department of the Unmasked. We are currently unavailable due to the protest on the corner of Virus Drive and Victory Lane. Please leave your name and number and we will be in contact with you: "In-contact" as "in-fected" and "in-noculated-not."

#5 Thank you for calling the Department of the Vaccinated. Our agents are currently mingling in the coffee room, content with their completion of doses of coffee, vaccines, and comfortable walking shoes. You may leave your number and an agent will be with you shortly, dispensing joviality.

#6 The Department of the Unvaccinated is not accepting any more calls at this time. All agents are out of the office, suffering from social anxieties, fearful of all surroundings, protesting six feet from everyone.

#7 You have reached the Department of Card Required. Our agents are eager to help you, but the workload to add regulations is increasing so rapidly we cannot take your call. Yes, you will need your card to enter any government building, eat in any restaurant, attend any social gathering, cross any state line, enter any store. No card/no social life/no mingling/ no touchy feely/no smoochin'/no lovin'......what's left to do?

#8 We are currently out of the office and cannot take your call. Leave a message and a counselor will return your call within the next decade. There are currently no positions available where no card is required. If you find one, please leave their name and address and we will be in touch with them for non-compliance.

If this is an emergency, you may attempt to contact:

Call: (new) nor-malcy (639) 667-62529 or email: nothingwill@ benormal.again

Thank you! Have a nice day.

Click!

THE SEVENTY SOLUTION

Jude Walsh

November 1, 2020, deep into the Covid-19 lockdown, was my seventieth birthday. My son died a year before, so it was just me and my three animal companions: Lottie Ann, a Yorkie and the boss of the pack, and two Coton de Tulear siblings, Lucie and Luckie. At that point, in my state of Ohio, we had been in lockdown since early March. The number of deaths in the U.S.—228,185—topped the world count. We were wearing masks and isolating. It was a lonely time for me. I had a nightly date with Netflix and Dove Chocolate (delivered by Amazon in 150-piece packages). I ventured to the grocery store only during senior shopping times.

I love celebrating my birthday, especially those when I embrace a new decade. My celebration plan for seventy included a trip to Bali, a long-anticipated destination, which was clearly a no-go. My favorite winter activity is attending college basketball games. The games would still be played but without spectators. The plays and concerts I held tickets for were all canceled. There would be no gathering at restaurants for birthday dinners. I ached with loneliness.

Despite the disappointment and underlying fear as I watched the deaths mount, I was grateful. I knew I was fortunate. I did not need to leave my home to go to work. I could afford to have groceries delivered if necessary. I was in good health. The local parks were open for socially distanced walking and hiking. I participated in numerous Zoom groups. Both of my formerly in-person writing groups continued to meet online.

Then, on my birthday, a wonderful surprise! Several of my writing-women friends surprised me with a socially distanced party on my deck! They appeared at my backyard gate, bundled in warm coats, hats, mittens, and masks. Though we could not touch one another, the physical proximity was exhilarating. We were as giddy as schoolgirls. They brought party hats, including a tiara for the birthday girl, decadent treats, and wine for a toast. There were party favors including cloth masks for everyone that read, "Plot, it builds character." They even had two candles, a seven and a zero to properly mark my age. It was much easier blowing those two candles out than seventy individual ones. At barely thirty degrees, we were freezing, abandoning the wine for hot tea and holding the mugs for extra warmth. And still, we talked and talked and talked. We were loath to part but when it began to snow, we knew the party was over.

Later that evening, alone again, I was journaling about the surprise party. I felt loved, seen, appreciated, and connected. I wanted to keep that feeling. I firmly believe that how we feel impacts our health and well-being. I started to make a list of all the details, the things that brought me joy. Writing them down, remembering them, helped me drop right back into feeling the joy in my body. I felt both relaxed and exhilarated. I could feel my heart swell. A shiver of delight rose from my toes to my head. I felt light, almost glowing. I could do it. I could bring forward that sensation at will. In that moment I vowed to make this a continuing practice, to pause and bring forth positive sensations.

I could use this technique to elevate my mood whenever I was lonely or fearful or sad. Now, I tag the entries in my journal that document extra special joyful moments.

In December, my godchildren video chatted with me to share their beautiful new son. I had long been praying for them to have a child and this little one stole my heart at first sight. He was gorgeous and his parents were radiating happiness. We were all crying and laughing and celebrating this miracle of love. My heart felt so full I thought it might burst from my chest. Definitely a feeling to revisit.

In January, I received my first vaccine. Vaccines were just beginning to be available, and appointments were hard to get. A friend tipped me off to a clinic that had an extra, late-in-the-day vaccine delivery. Driving straight there, getting an immediate appointment, and having a shot in my arm within an hour was incredible. After the injection, I felt my shoulders drop. I did not realize until that moment I had been clenching those muscles, probably for a long time. I cried happy tears. The nurses giving the injections appreciated my gratitude. My nurse said it felt so good to do something to prevent the virus rather than just treat infected people. I got my second shot in February and two weeks later, when I was considered fully immunized, for the first time in months, I felt I could finally, completely relax. Body relaxation is a feeling to recall.

By late March, all the people in one of my writing groups were vaccinated and the CDC said it was safe to meet in small groups without masks if all parties had completed their shots. We met at my home, did a simple carry-in meal, and even managed to do a little writing—that is, when we were not hugging one another. The room was filled with happiness, spilling out from each person and mingling into a golden cloud. How nice to see air charged with joy as opposed to the virus. My body felt free, light, buoyant. Yes, more of this!

As I write this, we are struggling with the Delta variant of the Coronavirus. I hope a booster shot will be approved in the near future. In the interim, I am again wearing a mask when in a public place. I am limiting my exercise to outdoor locations and am back to grocery shopping in the off-hours. Rather than being depressed or discouraged by this, I am feeling okay, resilient even. I credit part of this to my feeling technique, what I now call my Seventy Solution, honoring its discovery on my birthday. Whenever I feel down, I stop and take five or ten minutes to breathe deeply, revisit one of my joyful times, either from memory or from a journal entry. I concentrate on feeling it in my body, just like I did on my birthday. Reading, writing, and imagining joyful moments is my personal vaccine.

I am only a few weeks away from my seventy-first birthday. I am not yet planning how to celebrate. But I am looking forward to it. I know how I will feel on that day because I will either be making a new memory to add to my collection, or reliving one from the past. I will feel centered, and my body will vibrate with joy. I will carry my Seventy Solution with me for the rest of my days, not just for my birthdays or during a pandemic, but for always.

BE STILL AND KNOW
Marian McCaa Thomas

Teaching runs in my family: my husband is a retired chemistry professor, I teach piano and harpsichord, our eldest son is a math professor, our daughter is a preschool teacher, and our second son was a music professor, choral director, singer and composer. He was especially good at creating choral programs with a theme, and he wrote enlightening program notes. I once asked him where his creative ideas came from and he replied, "Mom, some things should remain a mystery!" He was at the height of his career when blood cancer struck.

From its diagnosis when he was 48 to his death two days before his 50th birthday, there were fourteen long months of shock, disbelief, hope, determination, the frustration of separation by 1200 miles due to the ongoing pandemic, and goodbyes via FaceTime. Like a yo-yo, we went up or down depending on the results of bone marrow draws, various chemotherapies, a stem cell transplant, and blood tests. The worst part was not being able to escape television coverage of COVID-19 patients tethered to ventilators in ICUs. I was constantly reminded of Steven's plight, even though the cause of his hospitalization was different. Because Steven loved the outdoors but was confined in ICUs for months, I sent him a twenty-minute video of twenty different morning birdcalls recorded in a British meadow. Even though sedated, he could enjoy hearing the "bird chorus," and his last email to me was a two-word response to the video: "Thanks, Mom!" My final words to him were also ones of gratitude for all the beautiful music he had created.

Steven and I had bonded through music. I was his first music teacher, and accompanied him when he played the clarinet. His boy soprano voice was lovely, and we sometimes played piano duets. When he was studying choral conducting, he shared tips with me on how to improve my choir-directing skills. We shared the thrill of visiting Bach's grave in Leipzig, Germany, and the very year I retired from being a church musician, I attended his conducting of Bach's *St. John Passion* with choir and orchestra. It was marvelous to know that my love of Bach would be carried on in his work. We both looked forward to his having my harpsichord and all my scores of Bach's keyboard pieces one day.

After Steven died, when my grief was overwhelming, I found strength in the words of the hymn, "How Firm a Foundation." In the third stanza, God speaks directly to the singer:

"When through the deep waters I call thee to go,
the rivers of sorrow shall not overflow;
for I will be near thee, thy troubles to bless,
and sanctify to thee thy deepest distress."

Howard Thurman wrote that when suffering arises, we should first feel our response to it and admit its hold on us, and then take it directly to God. And Joseph Campbell taught that everything that happens in one's life is a gift, a given beyond one's control, to be experienced to the full with gratitude. How in the world could I be grateful for Steven's death? I had been learning to meditate for many years, initially guided by readings of John Main, a Benedictine, in the company of my pastor. We meditated once a week for ten years, and after I retired I began meditating every morning. I thought of it as "my date with God." I used the Hebrew word *shalom* as a silent mantra, but sometimes I calmed my mind and heart by slowly chanting words from Psalm 46, like this: "Be still and know that I am God … be still and know that I am … be still and know … be still … be."

There are familiar biblical passages that use the word 'know' or 'known:' *I know that my Redeemer lives* (Job); "*O God, you have searched me and known me*" (Psalm 139); "*Now I know only in part, but then I will know fully, even as I have been fully known"* (1 Corinthians:13). In 2011, when she was 99 years and 5 months old, my mother broke a hip and was scheduled for surgery the next day. I was 1200 miles away, and telephoned her to say, "I love you, and I am praying for successful surgery tomorrow." Her response? Just two words: "*I know.*" The surgery did not happen, however, for later that evening she peacefully slept away.

In Celtic tradition, there are "thin places" where the veils between our world and other worlds open up to reveal eternal truths. Hallowe'en is an especially auspicious time for such piercing of the veil. Steven died on July 12, 2020, and I had a dream 3½ months later in the early morning of Hallowe'en. He is five or six years old, and is lying in a bathtub with his eyes closed, water covering his nose and mouth. I lean over and pick him up, feeling his heaviness. "Steven," I say, "Your nose and mouth were under water—I wondered if you were dead." He opens his eyes, looks at me, smiles and says, "*I know.*" He is very much alive.

A friend of mine interpreted the dream for me. She said, "the young Steven represents his energy and spirit, and he is smiling and peaceful because he died knowing he was loved." My mother and Steven both died peacefully because they knew they were entering fully into the mysteries of LOVE. They both lived intensely, fully, true to their natures. Although my mother's life was nearly twice as long as Steven's, both were as long as they were meant to be. As a freshman in college, Steven got to sing in Bach's *St. Matthew Passion*, and was so moved by the experience that he decided to pursue choral directing as a career. Thirty years later he led orchestra, double chorus and soloists in that very work for an annual Bach Festival in Pennsylvania. He had set a goal for his life, and had achieved it before he died.

Soon after his death, I wrote his birth and death dates in my journal followed by these words: *I say, "TOO SHORT!" but God says, "JUST RIGHT!"* It has taken time, but I have come to accept God's perspective on Steven's life. How has God sanctified the deep distress of Steven's death? One way is that a memorial fund has been created by the board of the Arcadia Chorale, which he directed. It will be used to give scholarships to undergraduate college students who sing with the Chorale and commit to educating the public about choral music. Many colleagues, former students, and choral groups will participate in a memorial concert to help raise funds, as soon as pandemic protocols make it possible. Another way I am being blessed is that I am continuing, at age 82, to learn new pieces by Bach, playing them on my harpsichord. Perhaps one of my grandchildren who is studying piano now will be the recipient of my instrument and keyboard scores one day.

Seven months after Steven's death, when my grief was still very strong, but when my faith that his spirit lives on was equally strong, I wrote the following poem:

> They say the day will come
> when thoughts of you will bring
> a smile
> before the trembling lips
> and tears
> rise up from an inner well
> of hopes dashed,
> of conversations ended.
>
> Some say to keep busy,
> for quietude lets
> my heart-held grief
> escape its hiding place
> to overwhelm
> my thoughts:
> I see your body
> lying on a simple bier
> awaiting cremation
> on your fiftieth birthday.
>
> Would I could
> truly celebrate
> your next adventure—
> free of pain,
> your Spirit
> joined with a mysterious muse,
> inspiring others
> to create the music
> which gave your life meaning.
>
> *I know* that day will come!

SMALL MOMENTS

Mary Jo West

One of my childhood chores,
dusting the furniture
was sidetracked by
coffee-table magazines,
I always sat down
to read.
Tuesdays, ironing day,
listening to rhythmic sound
of sizzling steam when
hot iron pressed hard
against clothes,
the sight and aroma
of freshly baked
chocolate chip cookies
cooling on the kitchen table,
snatching as many
as I could hold,
then dashing outside
to devour them all.
Mom cooking rich,
dark chocolate fudge,
then letting me lick the pan,
Mom's Irish temper
flaring up
when I pulled away
top half of sticky buns
covered with walnuts,
melted brown sugar and butter.
In times like these,
fluid memories,
blended from small moments
comfort me, resonating
how Simple could be and
can be again.

CAIRNS AFTER COVID

Patricia Daly

In the simplest definition of this Scotch-Gaelic word, a cairn is a pile of rocks, a human-made stack of stones. Cairns have been built for millennia on every continent. They have different meanings and uses, different sizes, and different structures. But all cairns have rocks in common, whether they are balanced and shaped, or piled haphazardly, whether composed of a few rocks or a few hundred.

Cairns serve practical and useful purposes, such as to set boundaries, to show direction, or to mark distances. They have been used as landmarks, to identify burial sites, and for ceremony. They can range in complexity from loose stone piles to precisely constructed works of art.

Whether stacked by one person or a group, cairns guide and communicate. They show the traveler which way to go, or they affirm we're on the right track.

Cairns witness to the presence of others and the connection we have with those who have gone before us on this path. They invite us into the community and encourage us to keep going, to trust.

Cairns share many messages, some of which include: *keep going, don't give up, you're getting there. This place welcomes you, honor it. We who have gone before you acknowledge your journey.*

Rock has staying power—it endures. Some cairns have a wobbly appearance, in spite of the way each stone is chosen and positioned, one atop another. Many times, the stone or rock is jagged and misshapen. It seems impossible that it could become part of a rising, fitted structure.

In our country, too, the past several years of pandemic, social unrest, and political division have shaken the earth beneath us and sent everything meaningful tumbling to the ground. Our society is like a shore covered with rocks of all sizes and conditions.

We have to rebuild our lives and our democracy stone by stone, patiently and persistently, until our cairns of love and care and meaning are balanced and beautiful once again.

The cairn I'm building imaginally is my vision of our country and my own life as we move ahead in a post-pandemic world.

The bottom stone doesn't necessarily have to be the largest or most smoothly formed. Yet, it does have to be strong enough to be the base of every other rock that follows. I'd consider this bedrock our constitution. Our democratic government starts here. On top of that, everything else is built upward.

Whether it's a cairn constructed from stones collected from a mountain or from the beach, or if the formation is built with rocks the size of boulders or huge granite slabs, the message of the cairn is the meaning you attribute to each stone.

On top of the constitution I would place a stone representing these seven important values we cherish in our society: liberty, self-government, fair elections and the right to vote, equality, individual freedom, diversity, and justice for everyone.

Next I'd position the uneven stone of racial equality. It's jagged and apparently misfitting, but it's got to fit within the whole cairn if it truly represents our society.

On top of that, I'll look for a big, bright stone of religious freedom. Without a channel through which each citizen is permitted to acknowledge their God and believe in love and forgiveness, it will be impossible for the cairn to become any taller.

Next to be selected is a heavy stone representing equal access to healthcare, education, employment.

And finally, at the top, perhaps the rock that completes the structure and holds it steady: a personal sense of belonging and achievement within this society, responsibility for its safety, and duty to respect every member.

It's a tenuous structure, almost fragile in appearance. Each building block depends upon the rest to remain standing. They're diverse, but necessary to each other.

Let's picture ourselves encircling the cairn with arms locked and a renewed commitment to tend to the healing of our country and our world. We've been pummeled with dangerous, metaphorical rocks upon our society, and by the unforgiving stones of a viral pandemic within our bodies. We are hurting, inside and out.

Let us choose meaningful stones and begin to build a cairn of hope and intention, no matter how fragile it appears. Rock endures, and so can we.

A FRAGILE SAFETY...

Hendrika de Vries

It's April 2021. My adult daughter and I hug for the first time in a year. For a moment before she enters my home, we linger on the threshold.

"We are vaccinated, we're okay, right?" my daughter, having just driven ten hours to see me, laughs as she hugs me again.

"We're safe," I whisper.

My eyes fill with tears. For a moment I remember my own mother whispering those same magical words to me. I was seven years old, and we had just narrowly escaped death in a mass shooting by Nazis at the end of WWII in Amsterdam.

How do we re-enter life after trauma, especially the trauma of a life-threatening global pandemic that kept parents, children, and grandchildren apart so we could be safe? I thought I would jump into action when fully vaccinated and the lockdowns lifted. I would travel again, visit my family, give parties, socialize with friends and attend book events. Instead, I feel a deep fatigue, a hesitancy that hides a fearful vulnerability and tears. My therapeutic training tells me that I am grieving. My enthusiasm and creative energy have disappeared.

The psychologist Adam Grant coined the word "languishing" for our feelings of emptiness and stagnation caused by the pandemic. But for me, I sense a deeper trauma. My sense of safety—an illusion perhaps—was snatched away from me this past year. The deadly Covid virus, with its ability to mutate at will, joined with a virus of hatred that split our nation and wounded our soul.

Before the Covid pandemic changed the world, I was filled with excitement and focused energy. My memoir had won four awards since its publication four months earlier, months during which I had been on book tours and visited high schools to talk to amazing young people about my story. My calendar for the year was marked up with scheduled trips for award dinners, speaking engagements at Universities, Jewish Centers, high schools, and bookstores across the country. I even had a Dutch translation and an interested publisher in the Netherlands of my childhood.

Then Covid-19 entered our lives. At first, I optimistically rescheduled all my speaking events. Surely by the fall the pandemic would be under control! But the deaths soared, and lockdowns shut the doors on our lives. My grown-up children and grandchildren, who live in other states, canceled their planned visits. Lunches, dinners, and coffees with friends were canceled as we hid in our individual homes. Vulnerability hit us all in different measures.

The really introverted among us did not mind the isolation so much. The lack of social expectations freed up their creative muse to write or paint. And all of us found ways to cope and somehow stay connected. Zoom and Skype opened doors to visual contacts with long lost family members and introduced even octogenarians like myself to new venues of communication—in work and play.

Vaccinations offered hope and gradually we moved out of the crises created by the pandemic. As mask rules were lifted, we came out of our homes and back to what we hoped would be a normal life. But wait, no. Instead of feeling freed and happy, I wondered why I kept tearing up. I grieved the loss of a precious year-and-a-half of my life and struggled with the emotional impact of a nation violently polarized and on edge. The world no longer felt safe.

As a young child I had known an unsafe world in WWII Amsterdam. We hid a Jewish girl, a secret that would bring death if revealed. But as an adult, my home in Santa Barbara had been my sunny bubble on the Pacific, where caring friends and colleagues affirmed the goodness of life. In the lockdown isolation, however, the pandemic and political unrest triggered memories of another time ruled by violence, prejudice, and hatred. I went into old survival modes where the silencing of my voice and being invisible meant safety. And even as the worst aspects of the pandemic abated, I now felt frozen on an emotional threshold, a liminal space between memories of a traumatic past and fears of an unknown frightening future.

Fortunately, I live close to the ocean. From the time that I was a teenage long-distance swimmer in Australia, the shoreline where the land and the ocean meet has always been my place of safety and reflection, a different kind of liminal space where the muse tends me. I take long walks, my bare feet in water and sand. I listen to the rhythmic sound of the surf. I watch seals basking in the sun on rocks and buoys and follow the pelicans in their flight formations as they skim the ocean's shimmering surface. The waves calm my fears, my bones absorb the sunlight, and my lungs breathe in the salty-clean ocean air. Mother Nature places no demands on me at the ocean's edge. For a brief time, all is well. I feel safe.

Safety! It's a strange gift, not much talked about except in its absence. For women it has seldom been safe to walk alone after dark, or even during daylight in some isolated areas. And dark-skinned people in many parts of the U.S. have never felt truly safe. When I was a little girl, it was not safe to be Jewish in Amsterdam, and not safe to hide a Jewish person as we did. The world fought a global war to restore that safety. We obviously want to feel safe, but how much do we truly value safety for others or even ourselves in a culture that places the right to own assault weapons, guns of war, above the safety of innocent children, who are traumatized and endangered in mass shootings.

When my mother was asked why she risked her life and the life of her child in WWII to hide a Jewish girl in our home, she responded that she hoped someone would do the same for her daughter if circumstances were reversed. She added: "Remember, not one of our children is safe unless they are all safe."

When I lean into our post-Covid tomorrow, I recognize the Covid virus also as a teacher reminding us of our interdependence. For if the pandemic has taught us anything, it is that a virus does not care a hoot about our ethnicity, skin color, or religious preference. It shows us that we had better act together—one for all and all for one. When we take responsibility for one another's safety, we create safety for all of us.

I linger on my emotional threshold at the edge of the ocean and let myself absorb the smells, tastes, sounds and sights of safety. It's a luxury, a privilege beyond words, beyond riches. After all, the rich do not feel safe, or they would not need to erect electronically guarded gates around their communities. The incoming tide soaks me with a rogue wave. I lick the drops of salty water off my lips. A little girl splashing in the water nearby shrieks at its chill and makes me smile. A Golden Retriever chases a ball thrown into the sea by its owner. I don't know which of the two of them is having the most fun. In the distance a larger wave now gathers strength. A young surfer climbs his board and tries to ride it in. A pod of dolphins swim by, enchanting me with their playful grace. I am filled with gratitude.

I am ready to step into the new normal of our Covid-era future, and I whisper a prayer: *Please let each of my words and actions help make our world a little bit safer for all—for all the children, and the animals and the breathtaking beauty of our fragile watery planet.*

REMEMBRANCE LESSON

Ann Haas

History marks us –
With stains
Still worn today

ABOUT THE CONTRIBUTORS

JAMUNA ADVANI – SAN RAMON CA
I am a resident of California. I have published a memoir, "The Letter," and a poetry book, "The Land of Dancing Deer." I have been a member of Story Circle Network for the last few years. My hobbies are reading, writing, travel, and gardening.

JANICE AIRHART – LEANDER TX
A former medical technologist, freelance writer and editor, high school science teacher and community college English professor, Janice is currently seeking a publisher for *Mother of My Invention: A Motherless Daughter Memoir.* Her memoir is about growing up without the mother who was institutionalized with schizophrenia shortly after the author's birth and who died in an asylum in 1966, when the author was 13.

ALLISON ALLEN – DRIFTWOOD TX
Allison is retired and living in Driftwood, just outside Austin. She's recently taken her first Story Circle Network class and already feels what a welcoming home it is for women hoping to grow in their writing life.

PAT ANTIIONY – FONTANA KS
Pat writes the backroads, mining characters, relationships, and herself. A recently retired educator and former poetry editor, she holds an MA in Humanities, poems daily, edits furiously, and scrabbles for honesty no matter the cost. A daily contender with bipolar disorder, poetry is both release and compulsion, mania and crash, as she strives for the balance beneath her Libra stars. Her work is published and forthcoming in multiple journals.

DR. LISA BARON – PITTSBORO NC
Lisa is a writer, teacher, therapist, and mentor. She has filled journals with poetry and reflections for many years. Her writing reflects her strong commitment to introspection, and has been published in Women In Higher Education, The New Social Worker, and Natural Awakenings. Her recent essay, "Musings on Perfection Inspired by Jane Austen," appeared in "Jane Austen: An Anthology of Thoughts

and Opinions," edited by Arlene Bice, 2020. Dr. Baron's website is: LisaBaronCreative.com

PAT BEAN – TUCSON AZ

Pat is a retired award-winning journalist, who lives in Tucson with her canine companion, Scamp. She is a wondering-wanderer, avid reader, enthusiastic birder, Lonely Planet Community Pathfinder, Story Circle Network board member, author of *Travels with Maggie* – available on Amazon, and is always searching for life's silver lining.

CAROL J. WECHSLER BLATTER – TUCSON AZ

Carol is a recently retired psychotherapist. She has published stories and poems in Chaleur Press, Writing It Real anthologies, Story Circle Network's anthology, Covenant of the Generations by the Women of Reform Judaism, and on 101stories.org. Her story, Writing About Writing, will be published in the Story Circle Network Journal. She is a wife, mother, and grandmother, and is ecstatic when she listens to her eight-year-old granddaughter read her creative storybook writings.

LIN M. BRUMMELS – WINSIDE NE

Lin earned a Psychology BA from the University of Nebraska and an MS in Rehabilitation Counseling from Syracuse University. She's a Nebraska-licensed mental health counselor. Lin has published poems in journals, magazines, and anthologies, and served as Poetry Out Loud judge at Northeast Nebraska's Regional Semi-Finals. Her poetry chapbooks are "Cottonwood Strong" and "Hard Times," a 2016 Nebraska Book Award winner. Her book of poems, *A Quilted Landscape,* was published in 2021.

CLAIRE BUTLER – CINCINNATI OH

I hail from Cincinnati, and have two nonfiction manuscripts nearly ready for release. I am a writer and an artist, painting oil on canvas. I have been published in several journals and two anthologies, and have been selling my art since 2007. My two fur babies, Tilly and Gigi, are always at my feet, whether at the computer or the easel.

SANDRA CAREY CODY – CHALFONT PA

Sandra grew up in Missouri, surrounded by a family who loved stories. She has since lived in various cities in different parts of the country and can honestly say she's found something to love in all of them. She currently lives in a small town near Philadelphia. She is the author of six Jennie Connors mysteries, two Peace Morrow books, and assorted short stories. http://www.sandracareycody.com

JOAN CONNOR — KERRVILLE TX

Joan lives in Kerrville, and also in her travel trailer, as she, Husband and Dog Ava spend summers in the Pacific Northwest. She is writing a Peace Corps (Mongolia 2011-2013) memoir (still untitled) to complete her MFA with Lindenwood University. Joan's interests are varied prose/poetry writing forms. When not tapping the computer keys, Joan spends hours as a novice fiddler, lifelong pianist, neophyte painter, and bicyclist along the Guadalupe River. Her blog is Jottings by Joan at https://jamajoanjottings.blogspot.com

PATRICIA DALY — LARGO FL

Patricia is a USA Today bestselling author and writer of creative nonfiction and spirituality. She has been published by Leaders Press, Story Circle Network, *The Sun*, and *Reiki News Magazine*. She has indie-published *The Women in His Life* and *Indelible Imprint,* both available on Amazon. Her new book, *The Deliberate Thinker,* was published in October 2021. She is retired in Largo. Connect with her at www.PatriciaDalyWrites.com.

CYNTHIA F. DAVIDSON — HOPE VALLEY RI

A member of SCN for over a dozen years, Cynthia is now a member of the board and on the faculty. A longtime expatriate and former CBS News journalist, she spent two decades as a pioneer in the global management field. She credits SCN membership with the support and skill development required to publish her first memoir, *The Importance of Paris*. SCN also inspired Cynthia to start facilitating workshops and writing groups that capture women's lived wisdom.

BARBARA DEE — SAINT CLOUD FL

I am a three-time published book author and also coach others. I write on leadership, writing, and life, and publish a free e-letter, "Carpe Diem!" My personal essay, "Sawdust," appeared in Story Circle's annual anthology. Poetry is how I journal, intimate and rarely shared. I'm President of Suncoast Digital Press and develop online courses like "Build-a-Book Master Class for First-time Nonfiction Authors." I live in Florida; favorite activities are kayaking, fishing, and reading…often on the same outing! https://barbara-dee.com/

HENDRIKA DE VRIES – SANTA BARBARA CA
Hendrika is the author of *When a Toy Dog Became a Wolf and the Moon Broke Curfew*, a memoir about her childhood in Nazi-occupied Amsterdam, which won the 2019 Sarton Women's Book Award. A depth-oriented family therapist for over thirty years, Hendrika used memory, intuitive imagination and dreams to heal trauma and empower women. As faculty at Pacifica Graduate Institute, she helped students explore their archetypal life patterns. Her website is: www.agirlfromamsterdam.com

DEBRA DOLAN – VANCOUVER BC CANADA
Debra lives on the west coast of Canada, is a long time (50+ years) private journal writer, and an avid reader of women's memoir. She has been a member of Story Circle Network since 2009 and is a self-described pluviophile. Debra enjoys deep conversations over red wine and candlelight, solo nature walks, and has self-published two books, *Writings and Reflections: 1958 to 2018* and *Writings and Reflections: Turning 50 in 2008* (*Walking the Camino de Santiago*).

PATRICIA E. EAGLE – ALAMOSA CO
Patricia maintains an unyielding commitment to excavating and acknowledging what is challenging and resilient about her life and the lives of others. In 2019, she published *Being Mean, A Memoir of Sexual Abuse and Survival* (She Writes Press). Growing up Texan, she has an undergraduate degree from the University of Texas-Austin and a Masters in Multicultural Education from the University of Houston-Clear Lake. Now she watches the Milky Way stretch across south-central Colorado skies. https://patriciaeagle.com

SHAWN ESSED – TANEYTOWN MD
I live in a small town in Maryland with my husband, three kids and two cats. I love sitting outside in the morning, and taking walks any time of day. I love nature and books and I consider most things in my life an adventure.

SARA ETGEN-BAKER – ANNA TX
A teacher's unexpected whisper, "You've got writing talent," ignited

Sara's writing desire. Sara ignored that whisper and pursued a different career but eventually, she re-discovered her inner writer and began writing. Her manuscripts have been published in anthologies and magazines, including *Chicken Soup for the Soul, Guideposts, Times They Were A Changing*, and *Wisdom Has a Voice*.

JEANNE BAKER GUY – CEDAR PARK TX

Jeanne, SCN's 2018-2020 president, is a speaker and veteran self-awareness reflective writing teacher. She's the author of *You'll Never Find Us: A Memoir*, the story of how her children were stolen from her and how she stole them back (She Writes Press 2021), co-author of *Seeing Me: A Guide to Reframing the Way You See Yourself*, and author of numerous anthology essays. Details about this avid walker, slow reader, and irreverent blogger are on her website: https://www.jeanneguy.com/

ANN HAAS – MOGADORE OH

I am a certified legacy writer/facilitator who has taught legacy writing at the local, state and national levels including training Family Practice residents at a local hospital. I established the legacy program at the local hospice and developed legacy writing tools for the memory impaired. My legacy writing specialties are blessings, six-word memoirs, reverse bucket lists, *en plein air* nature writing, and a storytelling method using a three-question memoir format.

PATRICIA ROOP HOLLINGER – WESTMINSTER MD

"Pat" was raised on a farm, and thus developed an imagination pondering the nature of the universe as plants emerged from seeds the size of a grain of salt. Words held the magic of stories. She sings words to her own accompaniment on the piano or organ. She is a retired Chaplain/Pastoral Counselor/Licensed Clinical Professional Counselor, who lives in a retirement community with her husband and their cat "Spunky."

MARION HUNT – BERKELEY CA

I enjoyed 25 years as an elementary school teacher endeavoring to instill my excitement for exploration, discovery, and mastery with young minds. My first love was writing, and I am pleased that some of my students went on to earn their livelihoods as writers and editors.

I am proud that my greatest joy helped craft their professional adult lives. Though I write mostly for friends, family, SCN, and myself, I wrote one article that was published in WOODWORK magazine.

MARY JARVIS – AMARILLO TX

I'm a retired librarian discovering all kinds of new and interesting things to do – including writing.

ZANETA VARNADO JOHNS – WESTMINSTER CO

Zan is the author of *Poetic Forecast: Reflections on Life's Promises, Storms, and Triumphs* (2020) and co-author in *Voices of the 21st Century: Resilient Women Who Rise and Make a Difference* (2021) and *Jane Austen: an anthology of thoughts & opinions* (2021). Her poems appear in "Fine Lines Literary Journal" and "OpenDoor Magazine." Recognized by the University of Colorado as one of its 2007 Women Who Make a Difference, Zan is a retired human resources leader.

ROSEMARY KEEVIL – WHISTLER BC CANADA

Rosemary has been a TV news reporter, a current affairs radio show host, and managing editor of a professional women's magazine. She has a Master's degree in journalism and is currently a journalist covering addiction and recovery. She is the author of *The Art of Losing It: A Memoir of Grief and Addiction*. Website: https://rosemarykeevil.com

JENNIFER KIM-RANKIN – SAMMAMISH WA

I am a teacher who formerly worked as a mechanical engineer and an elementary school volunteer. I am an avid reader and writer, and I have had a short story published in a Korean-American literary magazine, *Literary Realm*.

NIRMALA KSHATRIYA – LOS ALTOS CA

Nirmala is a bilingual author, who has been published in English and Hindi for the last fifty years. Her articles on parenting have been published in "Femina," and on Indian freedom fighters in the Hindi journal, "Dharmyug." She wrote a column on Dream Interpretation for "The Times of India." After being widowed in 2012, Nirmala moved from Bangalore to the US to be with her three children in the San Francisco Bay Area.

LEN LEATHERWOOD – BEVERLY HILLS CA

Len is the Program Coordinator for SCN's Online Classes program and current president of Story Circle Network. She has been teaching writing privately to students in Beverly Hills for the past 21 years. She is a nationally recognized writing coach as well as an award-winning author. Len has published work in flash fiction and nonfiction and has been nominated for a Pushcart Prize. Her blog, 20 Minutes a Day, can be found at <u>lenleatherwood.com</u>.

JANE GRAGG LEWIS – LAGUNA NIGUEL CA

Jane lives in Southern California, where she enjoys the near-perfect weather riding her bike, playing Pickleball, kayaking, or visiting the San Diego Zoo/Safari Park. She has published two books, *Dictation Riddles* (an ESL activity text) and a memoir, *A Jar of Fireflies*.

JAN MARQUART – AUSTIN TX

I began writing daily in June 1972 and I haven't stopped. Twenty-six books later, I am still planning my next books. My life has not gone as planned and without daily writing I am not sure how I would have gotten through it all or who I would have become. As a psychotherapist, I use writing as the primary tool for healing and it has never failed.

CLAIRE MCCABE – ELKTON MD

Claire quarantined in the borderlands of Delaware and Maryland with her partner, three cats, two dogs and a pandemic puppy. She is grateful for the many online writing communities that continue to sustain her throughout the pandemic. Claire is thrilled to return to teaching creative writing in-person at the University of Delaware. She holds an MFA in poetry from the Solstice Program.

MARGARET DUBAY MIKUS – LAKE FOREST IL

Margaret is the author of five poetry collections. Her CD, *Full Blooming*, has selected short poems and 3 original songs. She also created a personal writing guide using her popular poem, "I Am Willing." She was the 2013 Illinois Featured Author for the *Willow Review*. Her poems, photographs, and essays have frequently appeared both online and in print, and her blog includes 67 poem-videos: <u>http://www.fullblooming.com</u>

MERIMÉE MOFFITT – ALBUQUERQUE NM

Merimée has been a teacher for SCN and several times a judge in annual writing contests. She retired from teaching to focus on her writing and has published five books since 2013 (two reviewed by Story Circle Book Reviews). She has participated in community workshops, teaching here and there in Albuquerque, a city with a high per capita rate of poets and happy roadrunners enjoying the lack of traffic.

SALLIE MOFFITT – RED OAK TX

Sallie is a native Texan and an award-winning essayist and memoir writer. Her works have been published in essay collections, literary magazines, and trade periodicals. She resides outside of Dallas, where she enjoys gardening and bird watching.

ERIN PHILBIN – PITTSBURGH PA

Erin is married to Christopher Boyle and has two children. She loves reading, writing, and all manner of fiber crafts. She also loves silliness and adventures with friends.

CHARLOTTE PHILLIPS – HOUSTON TX

Charlotte is a novelist, short story writer, and blogger. With her husband Mark, she writes the Eva Baum mystery series. Charlotte's short stories have appeared in multiple mystery-themed anthologies from L&L Dreamspell to The Final Twist – https://thefinaltwist. wordpress.com/authors/ She holds a BS in Biology and an MS in Management, Computing, and Systems. More here: https://www. amazon.com/Charlotte-Phillips/e/B002BWWUGC/

CHRISTY PISZKIEWICZ – SPRING VALLEY OH

Christy grew up in Chicago and raised her three children in its suburb of Des Plaines. Moving to Ohio (2014) to be near her two grandchildren, she and her husband, Paul, now reside on a "Hobby Farm." Being a Beekeeper, she enjoys making fruit jams (some fresh-picked!) and exploring nature. Storytelling, writing down and making up stories, especially with her grandkids, is her passion. Sharing her love for God, she has taught parish religious education for more than forty years.

DOROTHY PRESTON – FITCHBURG MA

Dorothy has a degree in Communications/Media, and has worked in the publishing industry for over twenty years, including Prentice Hall/

Simon & Schuster, Houghton Mifflin, and Little Brown. Her debut memoir, *Getting Off the Radiator*, is available on Amazon.com. It is Dorothy's hope that she can share her journey with those having gone through similar ordeals, so they might learn that forgiveness truly is divine, and along with it comes peace.

MARLENE SAMUELS – CHICAGO IL

Marlene is an author, sociologist, instructor and lecturer. When not writing about sociology, her passions include creative nonfiction, flash nonfiction, photography, and her Rhodesian Ridgebacks, Ted and George. Marlene earned her PhD from University of Chicago, where she serves on the Graduate School Advisory Council. Her books include: *The Seamstress: A Memoir of Survival*, and more recently, *When Digital Isn't Real: Fact-finding Off Line for Serious Writers*. Visit her at: www.marlenesamuels.com

MADELINE SHARPLES – PLAYA VISTA CA

Madeline authored *Papa's Shoes: A Polish shoemaker and his family settle in small-town America* (historical fiction); a memoir in prose and poetry, *Leaving the Hall Light On: A Mother's Memoir of Living with Her Son's Bipolar Disorder and Surviving His Suicide*; and *Blue-Collar Women: Trailblazing Women Take on Men-Only Jobs*. She also co-edited *The Great American Poetry Show* anthology, and wrote the poems for *The Emerging Goddess* photography book. Her poems have appeared online and in print.

HUDSON SIERRA – AUSTIN TX

Hi! I am a Performance Theatre and Dance Major at McCallum Fine Arts Academy. My grandmother is Jeanne B. Guy, author of *You'll Never Find Us* and a fellow contributor here, and also the creator of a pretty cool mom. I've always loved writing and I'm finally learning how to take my experiences in a short sixteen years of life and put them into meaningful words.

SANDRA STANKO – KITTANNING PA

Sandra is a professional marketing writer turned lifewriter. Beginning her career in corporate communications, she currently works in post-secondary education and lifelong learning. Sandra specializes in journaling applications in the areas of nature writing, spirituality, and writer development. She is pursuing certification as a Pennsylvania

Master Naturalist and as a Certified Journal Facilitator through the Therapeutic Writing Institute. She has a PhD in composition studies.

DEBRA THOMAS – SIMI VALLEY CA

Debra is a writer, teacher, and immigrant/refugee rights advocate. Originally from Binghamton, New York, she has lived in Southern California most of her adult life. Her debut novel, *Luz*, won the 2020 Sarton Award for Contemporary Fiction and the 2020 Next Generation Indie Book Award for Multicultural Fiction. She is currently at work on her second novel, to be published by She Writes Press in Spring 2023. For more, check out her website: debrathomasauthor.com.

MARIAN McCAA THOMAS – LEAWOOD KS

I am a musician (keyboards and choral directing) and consider myself a "medial woman" (look up Toni Wolff's writing!) I enjoy reading and writing, gardening, maintaining friendships of long standing, and making new friends. I worry about what we are doing to our planet and to each other, and try to help combat climate change (solar panels on our house!) and work for peace and justice. I am almost finished writing my mother's biography, and hope to get it published soon.

JO-ANN VEGA – MILLSBORO DE

A lifelong educator and learner, eager to get back to in-person presentations and engage and share with others. Recently published a memoir, *Moments in Flight*, and working on a companion book of poems I've written over the past…wait for it…fifty years – which I hope to publish early in 2022.

JO VIRGIL – AUSTIN TX

Jo retired from a career in journalism and community relations. She has a Master of Journalism degree with a minor in Environmental Science, reflecting her love of writing and appreciation of nature, and has had stories and poetry published in various books, newspapers, and magazines, including Story Circle Network's publications. Jo lives by words she learned from one of her journalism professors: "Stories are what make us matter."

JUDE WALSH – DAYTON OH

Jude is an author, life coach, and writing teacher. As a coach, she works with women post-divorce and men and women wishing to reinvent themselves creatively and pivot to a new life. She teaches writing mindset and legacy writing. Jude is the author of the award-winning *Post-Divorce Bliss: Ending Us and Finding Me*. Her work is in numerous literary magazines and anthologies including *Chicken Soup For the Soul* and *The Magic of Memoir*. Find out more at: http://www.judewalshwrites.com and http://secondbloomcoaching.com

CHRISTINA M. WELLS – ANNANDALE VA

Christina is an editor and coach who lives in Northern Virginia. She has published in *Story Circle Journal, Northern Virginia Review, Crab Fat Magazine, bioStories, Big Muddy*, and *Sinister Wisdom*, among others. Her work is also in *Hashtag Queer Volume 3, Is It Hot in Here, or is it Just Me?*, and *Real Women Write: Living on COVID Time*. She has an MA from University of Arkansas and a PhD from University of Maryland. Find her online at www.christinamwellswriter.com.

MARY JO WEST – SAN CLEMENTE CA

I am eighty-one years old and have been married for sixty-two years. I have three daughters and nine grandchildren. I started writing nine years ago and during that time, I have published my memoir, *No Reservations*, and a recipe book of my Italian-American family's favorites that have been handed down for generations. Now I am writing free verse poetry and short stories.

JEANNE ZEEB-SCHECTER – VALLEY VILLAGE CA

I have been a homeopathic doctor for the past twenty-six years. During this pandemic, I retired. I belong to a local poetry class, a writing class, and I teach a Life Writing class. I joined SCN five years ago. Currently, I am writing a nonfiction book on Homeopathy and Grief, as well as a historical novel about a healer. I am blessed to be married, have a daughter, four granddaughters, and seven great-grandchildren.

THELMA ZIRKELBACH – HOUSTON TX

Thelma is a multi-published author of poetry, memoir, flash fiction and flash nonfiction, personal essay, and romantic suspense. She is also a recently retired speech-language pathologist. She is a native Texan, and shares her home with Cassie, her intelligent and demanding cat.

ARIELA ZUCKER – ELLSWORTH ME

Ariela was born in Israel. She and her husband left twenty years ago and now reside in Maine, where they run a Mom-and-Pop motel. Ariela writes poetry and nonfiction, offers online classes, and blogs regularly at Paper Dragon. https://paperdragonme.wordpress.com/

ABOUT THE EDITOR

SUSAN SCHOCH, editor of *Beyond COVID: Leaning Into Tomorrow,* is a freelance writer and editor specializing in personal history. She is author of *The Clay Connection,* a study of renowned ceramic artists Jim and Nan McKinnell for the American Museum of Ceramic Art. She also serves on the Board of SCN, reviews writing by and about women at Story Circle Book Reviews, and edited the 2017 SCN essay collection, *Inside and Out.* She has been editor of the annual *Real Women Write* anthology series since 2014. Susan lives in the Colorado foothills with her husband, Bob Smith, a ceramic artist and teacher. They have a large and loving family, cuffed by the pandemic but moving forward together.

ABOUT STORY CIRCLE NETWORK:
THE POWER OF WOMEN'S VOICES
ABOUT STORY CIRCLE NETWORK:
THE POWER OF WOMEN'S VOICES
Helen (Len) Leatherwood

"We learn best to listen to our own voices if we are listening at the same time to other women, whose stories, for all our differences, turn out, if we listen well, to be our stories also."
— BARBARA DEMING

As the president of Story Circle Network, I am delighted to share with you a bit about this wonderful organization's history, as well as information about our ongoing efforts to encourage all women to tell their stories. Having been a member of SCN since 2008, I feel honored to be part of a writing community that not only believes in the power of story but also encourage women to give voice to their life experiences, large and small, in whatever form of writing that works best for them.

SCN was founded as a nonprofit organization in 1997 by Susan Wittig Albert, a New York Times bestselling author or co-author of over 100 mysteries, historical and biographical fiction, memoir, and nonfiction. Susan was driven to establish SCN because of her deep-seated belief in the power of women's histories and the importance of women sharing their personal stories. This has been the mission of our organization since its inception twenty-four years ago. Over those years, SCN has had more than 4000 members from the US and around the world and has touched the lives of countless others through its many programs. As a nonprofit, we operate with a small paid staff and a large contingent of dedicated volunteers. Our funding comes from annual membership dues, program fees, and generous donations from grants and supporters.

Story Circle Network offers a wide array of opportunities and programs to help fulfill our mission. We provide online and in-person classes, monthly webinars, national and international writing workshops, a yearly virtual writing conference, a biennial in-person writing conference, virtual reading and writing circles, publication opportunities, and writing competitions. We also sponsor Story Circle Book Reviews, the largest and oldest women's book review site on the Internet, as well as the annual Sarton Women's Writing and Gilda Awards.

In addition, SCN is committed to diversity and inclusion and encourages BIPOC and LGBTQ+ women, and women with disabilities to join our ranks. This past year we partnered with College Match to mentor economically disadvantaged high school girls. We want to encourage *all* women to tell their stories.

One of our primary goals at SCN is to offer our members a variety of ways to publish their lifewriting, memoir, poetry, fiction, and nonfiction. Not only do we have two blogs, "Telling HerStories" and "One Woman's Day," but also publish our quarterly *Story Circle Journal* and the annual *Real Women Write* anthology in print and online. In addition, SCN has published four collections of members' and others' writing: *With Courage and Common Sense: Memoirs from the Older Women's Legacy Circle*; *What Wildness is This: Women Write about the Southwest*; *Kitchen Table Stories*; and *Inside and Out*.

I encourage you to learn more about this organization by visiting our website at https://www.storycircle.org. We welcome writers at all levels, from novice to expert, and encourage all forms of writing. We are ready and willing to provide guidance, support, and camaraderie to any woman who wants to add her voice to the chorus that counts Story Circle Network as a safe haven for sharing our stories with one another, as well as with the world.

HELEN (LEN) LEATHERWOOD
The current president of Story Circle Network and also the Program Coordinator for SCN's Online Classes Program. She has been teaching writing privately to students in Beverly Hills for the past 21 years. She is a nationally recognized writing coach, as well as an award-winning author. Len has published work in flash fiction and nonfiction, and has been nominated for a Pushcart Prize. Her blog, 20 Minutes a Day, can be found at lenleatherwood.com.

Books Published by Story Circle Network

Starting Points
by Susan Wittig Albert

Writing From Life
by Susan Wittig Albert

What Wildness is This: Women Write About the Southwest
edited by Susan Wittig Albert, Susan Hanson, Jan Epton Seale,
Paula Stallings Yost

Inside and Out: Women's Truths, Women's Stories
edited by Susan Schoch

Real Women Write, Vol. 18
Growing / Older
edited by Susan Schoch

Real Women Write, Vol. 19
Living on COVID Time
edited by Susan Schoch

Real Women Write, Vol. 20
Beyond COVID: Leaning Into Tomorrow
edited by Susan Schoch

Kitchen Table Stories
edited by Jane Ross

With Courage and Common Sense:
Memoirs from the Older Women's Legacy Circle
edited by Susan Wittig Albert and Dayna Finet

"Nothing in life is to be feared, it is only to be understood.
Now is the time to understand more, so that we may fear less."
—MARIE CURIE

This book was designed using Adobe Garamond, Copperplate,
and Eccentric fonts.
Designed and typeset by Sherry Wachter:
sherry@sherrywachter.com

Made in the USA
Las Vegas, NV
03 January 2022